J. Hudson Taylor.

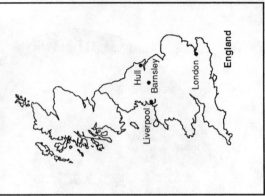

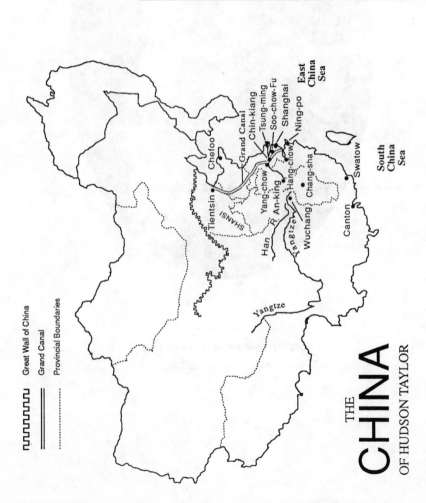

THE CHINA
OF HUDSON TAYLOR

Great Wall of China

Grand Canal

Provincial Boundaries

England

Hull
Barnsley
Liverpool
London

Tientsin

Chefoo

Grand Canal

SHANSI

Han R.

Yang-chow

An-king

Yangtze

Wuchang

Chang-sha

Canton

Yangtze

Chin-kiang
Tsung-ming
Soo-chow-Fu
Shanghai
Ning-po

Hang-chow

East China Sea

Swatow

South China Sea

Hudson Taylor's
Spiritual Secret

P U B L I S H E R S
BOX 3566 • GRAND RAPIDS, MI 49501

*PUBLISHING BOOKS THAT FEED
THE SOUL WITH THE WORD OF GOD.*

HudsonTaylor's Spiritual Secret

by Howard and Geraldine Taylor

Edited and Revised by Gregg Lewis

Hudson Taylor's Spiritual Secret

© 1990 by Overseas Missionary Fellowship

Published by Discovery House Publishers,
affiliated with Radio Bible Class, Grand Rapids, Michigan

Hudson Taylor's Spiritual Secret was first published in 1932 by the
China Inland Mission (now Overseas Missionary Fellowship). This
revision by Gregg Lewis is authorized by Overseas Missionary
Fellowship.

Library of Congress Cataloging-in-Publication Data

Hudson Taylor's spiritual secret / edited and revised by Gregg Lewis.
p. cm.

ISBN 0-929239-20-2

1. Taylor, James Hudson, 1832-1905. 2. Missionaries—China—
Biography. 3. Missionaries—England—Biography. 4. China Inland
Mission—History. 5. China—Church history—19th century.
I. Title: Lewis, Gregg A.
BV3427.T3H78   1990   89-48352
266'.0092—dc20 [B]   CIP

Printed in the United States of America

90 91 92 93 94 / CHG / 10 9 8 7 6 5 4 3 2 1

Contents

Foreword to the First Edition

This record has been prepared especially for readers unfamiliar with the details of Mr. Hudson Taylor's life. Those who have read the larger biography by the present writers, or Mr. Marshall Broomhall's more recent presentation, will find little that is new in these pages. But there are many, in the western world especially, who have hardly heard of Hudson Taylor, who have little time for reading and might turn away from a book in two volumes, yet who need and long for just the inward joy and power that Hudson Taylor found.

The desire of the writers is to make available to busy people the experiences of their beloved father—thankful for the blessing brought to their own lives by what he was, and what he found in God, no less than by his fruitful labours.

Howard and Geraldine Taylor
Philadelphia, Pennsylvania
May 21, 1932

Hudson Taylor's

Foreword to the Revised Edition

Over forty years ago, while visiting some Christian medical students in central China, I slipped out after an early morning prayer meeting and made my way along the bank of the mighty Yangtze River to the city cemetery in Chin-kiang. There I found what I had longed to see for many years: a gravestone with the simple inscription:

JAMES HUDSON TAYLOR — A MAN IN CHRIST

It was while reading the story of his life and work, when still a teenager, that I committed my life to serve God in China with the China Inland Mission, which Hudson Taylor had founded eighty years earlier.

Few biographies have had such an impact on the lives of so many Christians as *Hudson Taylor's Spiritual Secret*. It is a book to which people turn again and again with new inspiration and challenge each time they read.

But now it is available for the first time in a completely revised edition, and I am delighted to see that Gregg Lewis has made it accessible to today's reader. It addresses with even more relevance and immediacy the needs of those who seek a greater reality and effectiveness in their own spiritual lives, and it provides guidance and insight to those who are concerned about their part in God's plan for completing the task of world evangelization.

The story of Hudson Taylor reminds us of the continuing need for men and women of all nationalities who are prepared for a lifetime of sacrificial service. The principles demonstrated in his life—complete confidence in God's faithfulness and close identification with the people whom he served—must be the basis of missionary work today.

Hudson Taylor lived to see every province opened to the gospel through the arduous journeys of his fellow-workers and their Chinese colleagues. He was convinced that the evangelization of China must be accomplished by the Chinese church. The early pioneers planted and watered the seed, but "God made it grow," even when the foreign missionary was no longer present.

When the China Inland Mission withdrew from China in 1951 and started work in other Asian countries, its name was changed to the Overseas Missionary Fellowship. Together with many other like-minded mission groups, OMF seeks to witness to the truth so clearly established in this story of Hudson Taylor's life: "God's work done in God's way will never lack God's supplies."

David H. Adeney
Berkeley, California
Overseas Missionary Fellowship

Preface

When first asked if I'd be interested in revising and updating *Hudson Taylor's Spiritual Secret*, I almost reacted with a quick, "No thanks." I doubted that many readers today would be interested in a classic old biography of a nineteenth-century British missionary. And I wondered just how much there was in his story, however remarkable, that could be all that relevant as the world moves into the twenty-first century.

Then I read the book.

The going seemed a bit rough at first. It wasn't structured at all like a current best-seller. And the narrators' writing styles felt like an uncomfortable mixture of early twentieth-century camp meeting preaching and Victorian English Comp 101. As a result, the book seemed stiff, formal, and intensely "religious."

And yet as I read I saw unfold a truly remarkable story of a seemingly unimpressive man whose life and work made an impact on his world and time few figures in history—be they kings, generals, or presidents—could ever match. Hudson Taylor was indeed a significant man with an even more significant faith.

But what about any relevance to our world? Is Hudson Taylor's story really a book for today?

In our day, when the world closely and curiously watches every political and military development in the great country of China, this is the story of one Westerner who not only understood China, but changed its history. Millions of Christians in China today can trace their spiritual lineage to the life and work of Hudson Taylor.

In a day when the spiritual, moral, and financial failures of some of our culture's most visible Christian leaders have embarrassed the church and damaged the cause of faith, Hudson Taylor's story provides a startling, refreshing, and inspiring contrast. For it is a story of a Christian giant who led by serving, who diligently, carefully protected his integrity, who constantly, purposefully avoided personal material gain, and who refused even to take offerings in meetings where he spoke about his work—because he wanted to depend entirely on God's provision for both his personal needs and the needs of his ministry.

In a day when Christian missionary organizations around the Western world are striving for nationalization of their work, this is the story of a man whose mission organization held those goals more than a century ago.

In a day when much of the Christian church still debates the role of women in spiritual leadership, this is the story of a man who so respected the strength, potential, leadership, and faith of women that he ignored the conventions of his time to give unprecedented responsibilities and opportunities to the women of his mission.

This is the story of a man who understood the basic principles of "cross-cultural communications" a century before our communication experts began using the term.

This is also the story of a man in a formal, unemotional age who managed to be a romantic lover and an affectionate father. It's the story of a man who witnessed firsthand and battled against the major crises of drug addiction and homelessness. It's the story of a man who experienced the frustration of physical suffering and wrestled with the pain of personal grief. It's a story of one

Hudson Taylor's

man who discovered a faith and a secret that enabled him to accomplish the impossible.

Could Hudson Taylor's story be relevant to readers today? I decided it was.

But what about the book's troublesome style? The more I read of *Hudson Taylor's Spiritual Secret*, the more I realized that the problem wasn't the story itself; in fact, it had an almost epic quality—full of action and adventure (like shipwrecks and riots), overflowing with human emotion (like romance, despair, and grief)—with a setting as broad as the world, and a plot with as many up and down struggles as any first-rate novel.

The problem wasn't even the book's dated structure and dependency on the old journals and written remembrances of Hudson Taylor and those who knew him. In fact, there's not just a historical charm, but a sense of reality that comes through in those passages. The real challenge in getting contemporary readers to read *Hudson Taylor's Spiritual Secret* was the problem of accessibility. The book just seemed out of date and hard to read.

So my primary goal in revising the book was to make it more readable. In doing so, I've preserved the original book's basic structure, though I've divided some longer chapters and changed some chapter breaks in an attempt to make use of the most natural points of suspense in the story.

Virtually all the quotes from Hudson Taylor and his writings remain in this new edition. For even though his language is dated, his words carry a sense of raw honesty and power I chose not to tamper with. I even added some new quotes from Hudson Taylor's writings which I thought provided additional insight and interest for today's readers. These new quotes, like all those in the original *Spiritual*

Secret, were taken from a longer two-volume biography of Hudson Taylor written by the same authors—his son and daughter-in-law. And like the older system of spelling names of Chinese people and places adopted by Taylor, the original spellings are retained throughout. The authentic British spellings also have been preserved in all quoted text.

Most of the real revising of this book was done in the portions written by the story's original narrators. But even there I've attempted to maintain as much of the original as possible. My intention was to help new readers better understand the historical context of the story and to reduce the grating stiffness and formality without completely destroying the flavor and feel of the original Victorian style.

I hope and pray that in the reading you will be as inspired, challenged, and convicted by Hudson Taylor's life and faith as I was in working on this revision. For the original story is a powerful one—the story of a simple man with a powerful faith in a powerful God.

Gregg Lewis
Rome, Georgia

Prologue

More than a century before Richard Nixon reestablished diplomatic ties between the United States and China and opened up Communist China to the Western world, a young Britisher landed in Shanghai. Barely twenty years of age, he had no university degree. He was sent by no government official. He arrived unexpected and unannounced. No one came to meet his ship. No one in China even knew his name.

But Hudson Taylor was the man who opened the great country of China to the Western world for the first time. And the legacy of his life and work continues today in the lives of millions of people throughout China and around the world.

Hudson Taylor was not some holy hermit. He was a successful professional, a family man. He was a man of common sense, living a life of constant change in the company of many interesting and varied people.

He wasn't an imposing man at all. Small in stature and far from strong, he had to live with physical limitations. Next to a loving Christian family, the only real advantage he had in his early years was the experience he gained from supporting himself from the time he was about sixteen.

He was a hard worker, a trained medical assistant. He was able to care for a baby, cook a dinner, keep accounts, and comfort the sick and sorrowing. Yet he was also an innovative leader, an organizer, and a skillful delegator who provided spiritual leadership and inspiration to thoughtful men and women the world over.

Above all, he determined to test the promises of God. In doing so, he overcame difficulties few men have ever had to encounter. His life work changed the world he lived in and has had an impact on millions of people.

What was the secret of Hudson Taylor's life? What was it that enabled one man to make such a great and lasting impact?

That's what we're going to discover in the pages that follow.

1

---

*"I poured out my soul before God.
Again and again confessing my grateful love
to Him who had done everything for me . . .
I besought Him to give me
some work to do for Him as an outlet
for love and gratitude."*

1832 - 1850

James Hudson Taylor never appeared to be an exceptional child. Though his father had the education required to be a pharmacist, Hudson's parents decided not to send him to school until he was eleven. While he was a sickly child, missing at least one day of school almost every week because of illness, he quickly learned to read and showed a proficiency in math. But at the age of thirteen, after just two years of formal schooling, Hudson gave it up to help in his father's shop in the town of Barnsley, in Yorkshire, England.

Born in 1832 to devoutly religious parents, Hudson heard early and often the gospel story of Jesus, the only Son of God, who came to earth and died so that people's sins could be forgiven. And with a childlike faith, the young boy accepted what his parents taught him simply because they believed it.

As a teenager, however, Hudson began to question the reality of the Bible. And when, at the age of fifteen, he took a junior clerk position in a local bank and became exposed for the first time to the influence and opinions of older and more skeptical friends, Hudson abandoned the Christian faith and the teaching of his family.

Even after eye strain forced him to give up accounting and he again began working with his father, his doubts about Christianity continued. Though he wasn't outwardly rebellious, his parents recognized his spiritual struggle and worried about their son. Then, at age seventeen, something happened. Hudson later recorded the events of that day:

"On a day I can never forget . . . my dear mother being absent from home [visiting relatives some distance away], I had a holiday, and in the afternoon looked through my father's library to find some book with which to while away the unoccupied hours. Nothing attracting me, I turned over a basket of pamphlets and selected from amongst them a Gospel tract that looked interesting, saying to myself, 'There will be a story at the commencement and a sermon or moral at the close. I will take the former and leave the latter for those who like it.'

"I sat down to read the book in an utterly unconcerned state of mind, believing indeed at the time that if there were any salvation it was not for me, and with distinct intention to put away the tract as soon as it should seem prosy. I may say that it was not uncommon in those days to call conversion 'becoming serious'; and judging by the faces of some of its professors it appeared to be a very serious matter indeed! Would it not be well if the people of God had always tell-tale faces, evincing the blessing and gladness of salvation so clearly that unconverted people might have to call conversion 'becoming joyful' instead of 'becoming serious'?

"Little did I know at the time what was going on in the heart of my dear mother, seventy or eighty miles away. She rose from the dinner-table that afternoon with an intense yearning for the conversion of her boy; and feeling that, absent from home and having more leisure than she could otherwise secure, a special opportunity was afforded her of pleading with God on my behalf. She went to her room and turned the key in the door, resolved not to leave the spot until her prayers were answered. Hour after hour that dear mother pleaded, until at length she could pray no longer, but was constrained to praise God for that which His Spirit taught her had already been accomplished, the conversion of her only son.

"I in the meantime had been led in the way I have mentioned to take up this little tract, and while reading it was struck with the phrase, 'The finished work of Christ.' Why did the author use this expression?

"Immediately the words 'It is finished' suggested themselves to my mind.

" 'What was finished?'

"And I at once replied, 'A full and perfect atonement . . . for sin. The debt was paid for our sins, and not ours only but also the sins of the whole world.'

"Then came the further thought, 'If the whole work was finished and the whole debt paid, what is there left for me to do?'

"And with this dawned the joyful conviction, as light was flashed into my soul by the Holy Spirit, that there was nothing in the world to be done but to fall down on one's knees and accept this Saviour and His Salvation . . .

"When Mother returned a fortnight later I was first to meet her at the door and to tell her I had such glad news to give. I can almost feel that dear Mother's arms round my neck as she pressed me to her heart and said,

" 'I know, my boy. I have been rejoicing for a fortnight in the glad tidings you have to tell' . . . and went on to tell the incident mentioned above. You will agree with me that it would be strange indeed if I were not a believer in the power of prayer.

"Nor was this all. Some time later, I picked up a pocket-book exactly like my own, and thinking it was mine, opened it. The lines that caught my eye were an entry in the little diary belonging to my sister [who was four years younger], to the effect that she would give herself daily to prayer until God should answer in the conversion of her brother. One month later the Lord was pleased to turn me from darkness to light.

"Brought up in such a circle and saved under such circumstances, it was perhaps natural that from the commencement of my Christian life I was led to feel that the promises were very real, and that prayer was a sober matter of fact transacting business with God, whether on one's own behalf or on the behalf of those for whom one sought his blessing."

Without ever becoming the kind of "serious" Christian he thought so unappealing, Hudson tried never to take his faith lightly. Like most young Christians, he would sometimes fall to temptation and feel discouraged by his continuing weakness. But he never let himself feel satisfied with an up and down spiritual life. He longed for a better, more complete relationship with God, and one particular afternoon he began to pray about that longing:

"Well do I remember how in the gladness of my heart I poured out my soul before God. Again and again confessing my grateful love to Him who had done everything for me, who had saved me when I had given up all hope and even desire for salvation, I besought Him to give me some work to do for Him as an outlet for love and gratitude . . .

"Well do I remember as I put myself, my life, my friends, my all upon the altar, the deep solemnity that came over my soul with the assurance that my offering was accepted. The presence of God became unutterably real and blessed, and I remember . . . stretching myself on the ground and lying there before Him with unspeakable awe and unspeakable joy. For what service I was accepted I knew not, but a deep consciousness that I was not my own took possession of me which has never since been effaced."

Though he had committed his entire life to God, Hudson continued to struggle with times of failure and discouragement. And it was in one such experience of defeat and discouragement that he called out to God for help. He so wanted to live a life pleasing to God in every way that he felt he would go anywhere, do anything, suffer however the Lord asked if only God would give him the assurance of his clear direction.

"Never shall I forget [he wrote long after] the feeling that came over me then. Words could not describe it. I felt I was in the presence of God, entering into a covenant with the Almighty. I felt as though I wished to withdraw my promise but could not. Something seemed to say, 'Your prayer is answered; your conditions are accepted.' And from that time the conviction has never left me that I was called to China."

Hudson Taylor's immediate response to what he clearly felt was God's calling for him was simple and practical. From that day he began to prepare for a life that would call for physical endurance. He took more exercise in the open air, exchanged his feather bed for a hard mattress and carefully watched his diet. Instead of going to church twice on Sunday, he gave up the evening to visit in the poorest parts of town, distributing tracts and holding cottage meetings. In crowded lodging house kitchens he became a welcome figure, and even on the race course his bright face and kindly words opened the way for him to share his faith. The more he talked about God to others, the more he realized he needed to know. So he began devoting even more time to prayer and personal Bible study.

And of course, if he planned to go to China, he needed to learn Chinese. But a rare book of Chinese grammar would have cost him more than twenty dollars and a Chinese-English dictionary at least seventy-five dollars. He could afford neither. So he bought a copy of the gospel of Luke in Chinese. By patiently comparing brief verses with their equivalent in English, he uncovered the meanings of more than six hundred characters. These he learned and made into a dictionary of his own.

"I have begun to get up at five in the morning [he wrote to his sister at school] and find it necessary to go to bed early. I must study if I am to go to China. I am fully decided to go, and am making every preparation I can. I intended to rub up my Latin, to learn Greek and the rudiments of Hebrew, and get as much general information as possible. I need your prayers."

Several years working alongside his father in preparing prescriptions had given Hudson an interest in medicine. So when he heard that a physician in the seaside city of Hull needed an assistant, Hudson applied for the job and was accepted. Though this meant he had to move away from home, he was able to move in for a time with an aunt who lived in Hull and enjoy all the benefits of home.

Hudson's employer, Dr. Hardy, paid him a salary adequate for covering his personal expenses. The young assistant gave ten percent of his income to the work of God and devoted his own time on Sunday evenings to evangelistic work in the poorest part of town. And the more exposed he became to the needs of the poor he met, the more seriously he began to think about his own comfortable lifestyle.

If he spent less on himself, would he find even greater joy in being able to give more to others? Hudson decided to live out an experiment to try to answer that question.

On the outskirts of town, beyond some vacant lots, sat a double row of cottages bordering a narrow canal in a neighborhood referred to as "Drainside." The canal was really just a deep ditch into which the people of Drainside tossed their rubbish and sewage to be carried away with the tide.

The cottages, like peas in a pod, followed the winding drain for a half mile. Each identical house had one door and two windows. And it was for a rented room in one of these small shacks that Hudson Taylor left his aunt's pleasant home.

Mrs. Finch, Hudson's new landlady, was a true Christian and delighted to have "the young doctor" under her roof. She did her best to make the chamber clean and comfortable, polishing the fireplace opposite the window and making up the bed in the corner farthest from the door. A plain wooden table and a chair or two completed the appointments.

The room was only twelve feet square and was situated on the first floor of the bungalow, opening right out into the family's kitchen. From Hudson's lone window he could look across the drain to a pub whose lights were useful on dark nights shining across the mud and water of the drain.

In addition to his rather dreary surroundings, Hudson's move to Drainside required him to provide his own meals. This meant that he bought his meager supplies as he returned from surgery and rarely sat down to a proper supper. His walks were solitary, his evenings spent alone, and Sundays brought long hours of work, either in his new neighborhood or among the crowds who frequented the Humber Dock.

"Having now the twofold object in view [he recalled] of accustoming myself to endure hardness, and of economising in order to help those among whom I was labouring in the Gospel, I soon found that I could live upon very much less than I had previously thought possible. Butter, milk, and other luxuries I ceased to use, and found that by living mainly on oatmeal and rice, with occasional variations, a very small sum was sufficient for my needs. In this way I had more than two-thirds of my income available for other purposes, and my experience was that the less I spent on myself and the more I gave to others, the fuller of happiness and blessing did my soul become."

It was during this time at Drainside that Hudson gained a deeper, more painful understanding of the sacrifice that would be required to go to China. For it had been almost two years since he'd made the acquaintance of a talented and beautiful young music teacher from his sister Amelia's school. And Hudson had fallen in love.

Though the girl was a Christian, she didn't feel at all called to the mission field. On more than one occasion when they were talking about his plans, she asked Hudson if he couldn't serve God just as well at home as in China. But Hudson was sure of God's call. He was also deeply in love. And since she had never said she wouldn't be willing to go with him, he hoped and prayed that she would soon feel the same call he did.

But just weeks after he moved to Drainside, he got the final, heartbreaking word. She would not go to China. Hudson confided in a letter to his sister Amelia:

"For some days I was as wretched as a heart could wish. It seemed as if I had no power in prayer nor relish for it; and instead of throwing my care on Him, I kept it all to myself until I could endure it no longer."

Temptation gripped him, asking, "Why should you go to China, after all? Why toil and suffer all your life for an ideal of duty? Give it up now, while you can yet win her. Earn a proper living like everybody else, and serve the Lord at home. For you can win her yet."

Love pleaded hard. Then, as he told his sister:

"In the afternoon as I was sitting alone in the Surgery I began to reflect on the love of God; His goodness and my return; the number of blessings He has granted me; and how small my trials are compared with those some are called to endure. He thoroughly softened and humbled me. His love melted my icy, frost-bound soul, and sincerely did I pray for pardon for my ungrateful conduct . . . and had a wonderful manifestation of the love of God.

"Yes, He has humbled me and shown me what I am, revealing Himself as a present, a very present help in time of trouble. And though He does not deprive me of feeling in my trial, He enables me to sing, 'Yet will I rejoice in the Lord, I will joy in the God of my salvation . . .'

"Now I am happy in my Saviour's love. I can thank Him for all, even the most painful experiences of the past, and trust Him without fear for all that is to come."

2

" 'When I get out to China,' I thought to myself, 'I shall have no claim on anyone for anything. My only claim will be on God. How important to learn, before leaving England, to move man, through God, by prayer alone.' "

1851

"I never made a sacrifice," said Hudson Taylor in later years, looking back over a life that any objective observer would see as filled with self-denial. Yet he meant what he said because his experience had taught him that whenever he made any sacrifice for God, his compensation was so full and overwhelming that "giving up" seemed more like receiving.

And that was a lasting lesson he began to learn through some memorable experiences that winter at Drainside. No matter what sacrifice he made, the reward was greater. Despite the heartbreak of his lost love and an environment marked by bleak poverty, his spirit soared. He said, "Unspeakable joy all day long and every day, was my happy experience. God, even my God, was a living bright reality, and all I had to do was joyful service."

Even the tone of his letters changed—becoming less introspective and more focused on his plans for the future. China once more filled his thoughts. He felt and expressed even deeper concern for the spiritual condition of those who didn't know Christ as he did.

Yet despite his positive spirit, Hudson's mother worried about her son—his living conditions and his health. Especially after receiving reports from others that he looked pale and thin. When she wrote, asking about his health, he responded, in January:

"I am sorry you make yourself anxious about me. I think it is because I have begun to wear a larger coat that everybody says, 'How poorly and thin you look!' . . ."

He went on to assure her that he had recovered quickly from a bad cold and was now healthy and taking care of himself.

Evidently his mother wasn't completely satisfied. She even began to worry about the rigors of his planned missionary service to China. So he wrote again in an attempt to allay her concern about his present and his future:

"Do not let anything unsettle you, dear Mother. Missionary work is indeed the noblest any mortal can engage in. We certainly cannot be insensible to the ties of nature, but should we not rejoice when we have anything we can give up for the Saviour? . . .

"As to my health, I think I was never so well and hearty in my life. The winds here are extremely searching, but as I always wrap up well I am pretty secure . . . The cold weather gives me a good appetite, and it would be dear economy to stint myself. So I take as much plain, substantial food as I need, but waste nothing on luxuries . . .

"I have found some brown biscuits which are really as cheap as bread, eighteen pence a stone, and much nicer. For breakfast I have biscuit and herring, which is cheaper than butter (three for a penny, and half a one is enough) with coffee. For dinner I have at present a prune-and-apple pie. Prunes are two or three pence a pound and apples tenpence a peck. I use no sugar but loaf, which I powder, and at fourpence halfpenny a pound I find it is cheaper than the coarser kind. Sometimes I have roast potato and tongue, which is as inexpensive as any other meat. For tea I have biscuit and apples. I take no supper, or occasionally

Spiritual Secret   *15*

a little biscuit and apple. Sometimes I have a rice pudding, a few peas boiled instead of potatoes, and now and then some fish. By being wide awake, I can get cheese at fourpence to sixpence a pound that is better than we often have at home for eightpence. Now I see rhubarb and lettuce in the market, so I shall soon have another change. I pickled a penny red cabbage with three halfpence worth of vinegar, which made me a large jar-full. So you see, at little expense I enjoy many comforts. To these add a home where every want is anticipated, and 'the peace of God which passeth all understanding' and if I were not happy and contented I should deserve to be miserable.

"Continue to pray for me, dear Mother. Though comfortable as regards temporal matters, and happy and thankful, I feel I need your prayers . . . Oh, Mother, I cannot tell you, I cannot describe how I long to be a missionary; to carry the Glad Tidings to poor, perishing sinners; to spend and be spent for Him who died for me! . . . Think, Mother, of twelve millions—a number so great it is impossible to realise it—yes, twelve million souls in China, every year, passing without God and without hope into eternity . . . Oh, let us look with compassion on this multitude! God has been merciful to us; let us be like Him . . .

"I must conclude. Would you not give up all for Jesus who died for you? Yes, Mother I know you would. God be with you and comfort you. Must I leave as soon as I can save money enough to go? I feel as if I could not live if something is not done for China."

Yet even though Hudson longed to go to the Orient and to go at once, he wasn't entirely sure he was ready for the challenge. He wrote more of that winter in the little room in Drainside:

"To me it was a very grave matter to contemplate going out to China, far from all human aid, there to depend on the living God alone for protection, supplies, and help of every kind. I felt that one's spiritual muscles required strengthening for such an undertaking. There was no doubt that if faith did not fail, God would not fail. But what if one's faith should prove insufficient? I had not at that time learned that even 'if we believe not, yet he abideth faithful; he cannot deny himself.' It was consequently a very serious matter to my mind, not whether He was faithful, but whether I had strong enough faith to warrant my embarking on the enterprise set before me.

" 'When I get out to China,' I thought to myself, 'I shall have no claim on anyone for anything. My only claim will be on God. How important to learn, before leaving England, to move man, through God, by prayer alone.' "

Hudson Taylor believed what the Bible said: that faith could move mountains. But he wondered if his faith was yet strong enough to do the job. If it needed to grow, he decided he ought to exercise it. So that's what he did.

"To learn, before leaving England, to move man, through God, by prayer alone." That was his goal. And before long he came to see a simple, natural way to practice this exercise of his faith. He wrote of this lesson:

"At Hull my kind employer wished me to remind him whenever my salary became due. This I determined not to do directly, but to ask that God would bring the fact to his recollection, and thus encourage me by answering prayer.

"At one time, as the day drew near for the payment of a quarter's salary, I was as usual much in prayer about it. The time arrived but Dr. Hardey made no allusion to the matter. I continued praying. Days passed on and he did not remember, until at length on settling up my weekly accounts on Saturday night, I found myself possessed of only one remaining coin—a half-crown piece. Still, I had hitherto known no lack, and I continued praying.

"That Sunday was a very happy one. As usual my heart was full and brimming over with blessing. After attending divine service in the morning, my afternoons and evenings were taken up with Gospel work in the various lodging-houses I was accustomed to visit in the lowest part of the town. At such times it almost seemed to me as if heaven were begun below, and that all that could be looked for was an enlargement of one's capacity for joy, not a truer filling than I possessed.

"After concluding my last service about ten o'clock that night, a poor man asked me to go and pray with his wife, saying she was dying. I readily agreed, and on the way asked him why he had not sent for the priest, as his accent told me he was an Irishman. He had done so, he said, but the priest refused to come without payment of eighteen pence, which the man did not possess as the family was starving. Immediately it occurred to my mind that all the money I had in the world was the solitary half-crown, and that it was in one coin; moreover, that while the basin of water-gruel I usually took for supper was awaiting me, and there was sufficient in the house for breakfast in the morning, I certainly had nothing for dinner the next day.

"Somehow or other there was at once a stoppage in the flow of joy in my heart. But instead of reproving myself I began to reprove the poor man, telling him that it was very wrong to have allowed matters to get into such a state as he described, and that he ought to have applied to the retrieving officer. His answer was that he had done so, and was told to come at eleven o'clock the next morning, but that he feared his wife might not live into the night.

" 'Ah,' thought I, 'if only I had two shillings and a sixpence instead of this half-crown, how gladly I would give these poor people a shilling!' But to part with the half-crown was far from my thoughts. I little dreamed that the truth of the matter simply was that I could trust God plus one-and-sixpence, but was not prepared to trust Him only, without any money at all in my pocket.

"My conductor led me into a court, down which I followed him with some degree of nervousness. I had found myself there before, and at my last visit had been roughly handled . . . Up a miserable flight of stairs into a wretched room he led me, and oh what a sight there presented itself! Four or five children stood about, their sunken cheeks and temples telling unmistakably the story of slow starvation, and lying on a wretched pallet was a poor, exhausted mother, with a tiny infant thirty-six hours old, moaning rather than crying at her side.

" 'Ah!' Thought I, 'If I had two shillings and a sixpence, instead of a half-crown, how gladly should they have one-and-sixpence of it.' But still a wretched unbelief prevented me from obeying the impulse to relieve their distress at the cost of all I possessed.

"It will scarcely seem strange that I was unable to say much to comfort these poor people. I needed comfort myself. I began to tell them, however, that they must not be cast down; that though their circumstances were very distressing there was a kind and loving Father in heaven. But something within me cried, 'You hypocrite! Telling these unconverted people about a kind and loving Father in heaven, and not prepared yourself to trust Him without half-a-crown.'

"I nearly choked. How glad would I have compromised with conscience, if I had a florin and a sixpence! I would have given the florin thankfully and kept the rest. But I was not yet prepared to trust in God alone, without the sixpence.

"To talk was impossible under these circumstances, yet strange to say I thought I should have no difficulty in praying. Prayer was a delightful occupation in those days. Time thus spent never seemed wearisome and I knew no lack of words. I seemed to think that all I should have to do would be to kneel down and pray, and that relief would come to them and to myself together.

" 'You asked me to come and pray with your wife,' I said to the man; 'let us pray.' And I knelt down.

"But no sooner had I opened my lips with 'Our Father who art in heaven,' than conscience said within, 'Dare you mock God? Dare you kneel down and call Him 'Father' with that half-crown in your pocket?'

"Such a time of conflict then came upon me as I had never experienced before. How I got through that form of prayer I know not, and whether the words uttered were connected or disconnected. But I arose from my knees in great distress of mind.

"The poor father turned to me and said, 'You see what a terrible state we are in, sir. If you can help us, for God's sake do!'

"At that moment the word flashed into my mind, 'Give to him that asketh of thee.' And in the word of a King there is power.

"I put my hand into my pocket and, slowly drawing out the half-crown, gave it to the man, telling him that it might seem a small matter for me to relieve them, seeing that I was comparatively well off, but in that parting with that coin I was giving him my all; but that what I had been trying to tell them was indeed true, God really was a Father and might be trusted. And how the joy came back in full tide to my heart! I could say anything and feel it then, and the hindrance to blessing was gone—gone, I trust, forever.

"Not only was the poor woman's life saved, but my life as I fully realised had been saved too. It might have been a wreck—would have been, probably, as a Christian life—had not grace at that time conquered and the striving of God's Spirit been obeyed.

"I well remembered that night as I went home to my lodgings how my heart was as light as my pocket. The dark, deserted streets resounded with a hymn of praise that I could not restrain. When I took my basin of gruel before retiring, I would not have exchanged it for a prince's feast. Reminding the Lord as I knelt at my bedside of His own Word, 'He that giveth to the poor lendeth to the Lord,' I asked Him not to let my loan be a long one, or I should have no dinner the next day. And with peace within and peace without, I spent a happy, restful night.

"Next morning my plate of porridge remained for breakfast, and before it was finished the postman's knock was heard at the door. I was not in the habit of receiving letters on Monday, as my parents and most of my friends refrained from posting on Saturday, so that I was somewhat surprised when the landlady came in holding a letter or packet in her wet hand covered by her apron. I looked at the letter, but could not make out the handwriting. It was either a strange hand or a feigned one, and the postmark was blurred. Where it came from I could not tell. On opening the envelope I found nothing written within, but inside a sheet of blank paper was folded a pair of kid gloves from which, as I opened them in astonishment, half-a-sovereign fell to the ground.

" 'Praise the Lord,' I exclaimed, 'four hundred

percent for a twelve hours' investment! How glad the merchants of Hull would be if they could lend their money at such a rate of interest!' Then and there I determined that a bank that could not break should have my savings or earnings as the case might be, a determination I have not yet learned to regret.

"I cannot tell you how often my mind has recurred to this incident, or all the help it has been to me in circumstances of difficulty. If we are faithful to God in little things, we shall gain experience and strength that will be helpful to us in the more serious trials of life."

But this was not the end of the story. Nor was it the only answer to prayer that was to confirm the strength and readiness of Hudson's faith at that time. The conclusion of the story is told in his words:

"This remarkable and gracious deliverance was a great joy to me as well as a strong confirmation of faith. But of course ten shillings, however economically used, will not go very far, and it was none the less necessary to continue in prayer, asking that the larger supply which was still due might be remembered and paid. All my petitions, however, appeared to remain unanswered, and before a fortnight elapsed I found myself pretty much in the same position that I had occupied on the Sunday night already made so memorable. Meanwhile I continued pleading with God, more and more earnestly, that He would Himself remind Dr. Hardey that my salary was due.

"Of course it was not want of money that distressed me. That could have been had at any time for the asking. The question uppermost in my mind was, 'Can I go to China, or will my want of faith and power with God prove so serious an obstacle as to preclude my entering upon this much prized service?'

"As the week drew to a close I felt exceedingly embarrassed. There was not only myself to consider. On Saturday night a payment would be due to my Christian landlady, which I knew she could not dispense with. Ought I not, for her sake, to speak about the matter of the salary? Yet to do so would be, to myself at any rate, the admission that I was not fitted to undertake a missionary enterprise. I gave nearly the whole of Thursday and Friday, all the time not occupied in my necessary employment, to earnest wrestling with God in prayer. But still on Saturday morning I was in the same position as before. And now my earnest cry was for guidance as to whether I should still continue to wait the Father's time. As far as I could judge, I received the assurance that to wait His time was best, and that God in some way or another would interpose on my behalf. So I waited, my heart being now at rest and the burden gone.

"About five o'clock that Saturday afternoon, when Dr. Hardey had finished writing his prescriptions, his last circuit for the day being done, he threw himself back in his armchair as he was wont and began to speak of the things of God. He was a truly Christian man, and many seasons of happy fellowship we had together. I was busily watching at the time a pan in which a decoction was boiling that required a good deal of attention. It was indeed fortunate for me that it was so, for without any obvious connection with what had been going on, all at once he said: 'By the by, Taylor, is not your salary due again?'

"My emotion may be imagined. I had to swallow two or three times before I could answer. With my eye fixed on the pan and my back to the doctor, I told him as quietly as I could that it was overdue some little time. How thankful I felt at that moment! God surely had heard my prayer and caused him in this time of great need to remember the salary, without any word or suggestion from me.

" 'Oh, I am so sorry you did not remind me,' he replied. 'You know how busy I am. I wish I had thought of it a little sooner, for only this afternoon I sent all the money I had to the bank. Otherwise I would pay you at once.'

"It is impossible to describe the revulsion of feeling caused by this unexpected statement. I knew not what to do. Fortunately for me the pan boiled up and I had a good reason for rushing with it from the room. Glad indeed I was to keep out of sight until after Dr. Hardey had returned to his house, and most thankful that he had not perceived my emotion.

"As soon as he was gone, I had to seek my little sanctum and pour out my heart before the Lord before calmness, and more than calmness, thankfulness and joy were restored. I felt that God had His own way and was not going to fail me. I had sought to know His will early in the day, and as far as I could judge had received guidance to wait patiently. And now God was going to work for me in some other way.

"That evening was spent, as my Saturday evenings usually were, in reading the Word and preparing the subject on which I expected to speak in the various lodging-houses on the morrow. I waited perhaps a little longer than usual. At last about ten o'clock I put on my overcoat and was preparing to leave for home, rather thankful to know that by that time I should have to let myself in with the latchkey, as my landlady retired early. There was certainly no help for that night. But perhaps God would interpose for me by Monday, and I might be able to pay my landlady early in the week the money I would have given her before, had it been possible.

"Just as I was about to turn down the gas, I heard the doctor's step in the garden that lay between the dwelling-house and surgery. He was laughing to himself heartily, as though greatly amused. Entering the surgery he asked for the ledger, and told me that, strange to say, one of his richest patients had just come to him to pay his doctor's bill. Was it not an odd thing to do! It never struck me that it might have any bearing on my case, or I might have been embarrassed. Looking at it simply from the position of an uninterested spectator, I also was highly amused that a man rolling in wealth should come after ten o'clock at night to pay a bill which he could any day have met by a cheque with the greatest ease. It appeared that, somehow or another, he could not rest with this on his mind, and had been constrained to come at that unusual hour to discharge his liability.

"The account was duly receipted in the ledger and Dr. Hardey was about to leave, when suddenly he turned and, handing me some of the banknotes just received, said to my surprise and thankfulness: 'By the by, Taylor, you might as well take these notes. I have no change, but can give you the balance next week.'

"Again I was left, my feelings undiscovered, to go back to my little closet and praise the Lord with a joyful heart that after all I might go to China."

3

---

*". . . I felt I could not go to China without
having still further developed and tested my
power to rest upon His faithfulness . . ."*

1852 - 1853

With the impatience of an idealistic nineteen-year-old, Hudson wrote his sister a letter in March, 1852, in which he said:

"I feel I have not long to stay in this country now. I do not know what turn Providence is about to take, but I think some change is coming, and I am forewarned that I should be prepared. Pray for me that my faith shall not fail . . ."

Hudson saw no likely prospect for any immediate service with a missionary agency—they all required ordination and more training than he had. So he began to think of saving enough money to pay his own way to China; he would just trust God for provision once he was there. But even the thought of working to save up money for his own passage seemed an unacceptable and frustrating delay. So he began considering yet another alternative which he raised in that same letter to his sister:

". . . if I stay here another two years and save fifty or sixty pounds to pay my expenses to China, I shall land there no better off than if I go at once and work my passage out. In two years there will die in that land at least 24 million people . . . In six or eight months I should be able to talk a little Chinese. And if I could instruct in the truths of the Gospel one poor sinner . . . then what would the hardships of a four or five months' voyage weigh in comparison?"

27

Hudson hoped to find a berth as an assistant to a ship's surgeon. If that wasn't possible, he'd go as a sailor. Though he was more than willing to endure the hardship which that would entail, the advice and prayers of family and friends convinced him that he had more to learn before he set sail for the other side of the world.

Dr. Hardey offered Hudson a medical apprenticeship. But his plan required a commitment that would last several years. And as eager as Hudson was to become a doctor, he felt he needed to be ready to go to China as soon as the opportunity opened up. So he turned down the kind doctor's offer.

Shortly following, just months after his twentieth birthday, Hudson decided to continue his medical studies in London. He felt certain that after a short time there, the way would open to go to China. And he wasn't nearly as concerned about needing more money, more education, or even more maturity, as he was about continuing to exercise and strengthen his faith.

". . . I felt I could not go to China without having still further developed and tested my power to rest upon His faithfulness; and a marked opportunity for doing so was providentially afforded me.

"My dear father had offered to bear all the expenses of my stay in London. I knew, however, that, owing to recent losses, it would mean a considerable sacrifice for him to undertake this just when it seemed necessary for me to go forward. I had recently become acquainted with the Committee of the Chinese Evangelisation Society . . . and not knowing of my father's proposition, the Committee also kindly offered to bear my expense while in London. When these proposals were first made to me, I was not quite clear as to what I ought to do, and in writing to my

Hudson Taylor's

father and the secretaries, told them that I would take a few days to pray about the matter before deciding any course of action. I mentioned to my father that I had had this offer from the Society, and told the secretaries also of his proffered aid.

"Subsequently, while waiting upon God in prayer for guidance, it became clear to my mind that I could without difficulty decline both offers. The secretaries of the Society would not know that I had cast myself wholly on God for supplies, and my father would conclude that I had accepted the other offer. I therefore wrote, declining both, and felt that without any one having either care or anxiety on my account I was simply in the hands of God, and that He who knew my heart, if He wished to encourage me to go to China, would bless my effort to depend upon Him alone at home."

Hudson did accept the mission society's offer to cover his fees at the London Hospital where he studied, and an uncle in Soho gave him a place to stay for a few weeks until he could find permanent lodging. But beyond that, Hudson Taylor, a small-town boy, was on his own in the hustle and bustle of London.

Before leaving Hull he had written to his mother:

"I am indeed proving the truth of that word, 'Thou wilt keep him in perfect peace whose mind is stayed on thee, because he trusteth in thee.' My mind is quite as much at rest as, nay more than, it would be if I had a hundred pounds in my pocket. May He keep me ever thus, simply depending on Him for every blessing, temporal as well as spiritual."

About his search for a job that would pay living expenses and leave time for his studies, he wrote to his sister Amelia:

"No situation has turned up in London that will suit me, but I am not concerned about it, as HE is 'the same yesterday, and to day, and for ever.' His love is unfailing, His Word unchangeable, His power ever the same; therefore the heart that trusts Him is kept in 'perfect peace' . . . I know He tries me only to increase my faith, and that is all in love. Well, if He is glorified, I am content."

Hudson decided that if his faith were going to fail him, better to make that discovery in London than in China. So he continued his test, living on his meager savings and God's provision. He wrote of this time:

"To lessen expenses, I shared a room with a cousin, four miles from the hospital, providing my own board; and after various experiments I found that the most economical way was to live almost exclusively on brown bread and water. Thus I was able to make the means that God gave me last as long as possible. Some of my expenses I could not diminish, but my board was largely in my control. A large twopenny loaf of brown bread, purchased daily on my long walk from the hospital, furnished me with supper and breakfast; and on this diet with a few apples for lunch I managed to walk eight or nine miles a day, besides being a good deal on foot attending the practise of the hospital . . ."

The following months further tested Hudson's patience. Even as he studied, he prayed for an open door to China. During that time he almost died of a fever contracted from a cadaver he and fellow students worked on at the hospital.

But events were transpiring on the other side of the world that promised to change the course of Chinese history and suddenly made Hudson Taylor's long-time dream an immediate reality.

In China the Taiping Rebellion looked to be on the

verge of success. Its capital firmly established at Nanking, its nominally Christian forces had swept over the central and northern provinces. Peking itself looked almost within their grasp.

Hung Hsiu-ch'uan, founder of the Taiping movement, had read a Christian tract and been impressed with Christian teaching. He wrote to an American missionary, "Send me teachers, many teachers to help in making known the Truth. Hereafter, when my enterprise is successfully terminated, I will disseminate the Doctrine throughout the whole Empire, that all may return to the one Lord and worship the true God only. This is what my heart earnestly desires."

Suddenly, it seemed to the waiting Western world that China, closed for centuries to foreigners, was about to be thrown open to messengers of Christianity. The entire Christian church in Europe and North America grew excited at the prospect. It seemed an opportunity too wonderful to miss. Money began pouring in to the treasuries of mission organizations for China-related projects.

For example, the British and Foreign Bible Society decided to undertake an unprecedented printing of one million copies of the Chinese New Testament. And the society paying Hudson's school expenses decided to send two men to Shanghai as soon as possible. One of these men, a Scottish physician, couldn't leave immediately. But they thought Hudson Taylor, single and only twenty-one, might go on short notice, even if it meant sacrificing the degrees he was pursuing in medicine and surgery.

Despite his past impatience, the decision wasn't an easy one for Hudson. He had had enough dealings with the Chinese Evangelisation Society to realize some of what it would mean to be accountable to its organizers. He would need their approval for everything he did in China. They wanted to send him to Shanghai, but what happened if the way opened for him to move into the interior? He began to feel that God was calling him to inland China where no Western missionary had ever gone. And now with the seeming success of the Taiping Rebellion, the opportunity might be there.

He began to wonder whether or not he would be better off returning to his earlier plan of going to China on his own, dependent on and accountable only to God. He asked his friends and family for counsel and prayer in his decision. But after an interview with one of the secretaries of the society he wrote to his mother:

"Mr. Bird has removed most of the difficulties I have been feeling, and I think it will be well to comply with his suggestion and at once propose myself to the committee. I shall await your answer, however, and rely upon your prayers. If I should be accepted to go at once, would you advise me to come home before sailing? I long to be with you once more, and I know you would naturally wish to see me; but I almost think it would be easier for us not to meet, than having met to part again forever. No, not forever!

". . . I cannot write more, but hope to hear from you as soon as possible. Pray much for me. It is easy to talk of leaving all for Christ, but when it comes to the proof—it is only as we stand 'complete in Him' we can go through with it. God be with you and bless you, my own dear Mother, and give you so to realise the preciousness of Jesus that you may wish for nothing but 'to know him' . . ."

And to his sister he wrote:

"Pray for me, dear Amelia, that He who has promised

to meet all our need may be with me in this painful though long-expected hour."

The decision was soon made: Hudson Taylor was going to China. And he booked passage on the first ship he could find.

. . .

Moored at her landing in a Liverpool dock, the double-masted sailing ship, *Dumfries*, was bound for China. A small vessel of 470 tons, she was carrying only one passenger. So there was no crowd to see her off.

Mr. Pearse, a representative of the mission society, and Hudson's father had made the trip to Liverpool. But when needed repairs delayed the ship's departure they both had to return home, leaving only Hudson's mother to actually see him off. He later recalled the difficulty of that exciting and sad experience:

"On the 19th of September, 1853, a little service was held in the stern cabin of the *Dumfries* which had been secured for me by the Chinese Evangelisation Society, under whose auspices I was going to China.

"My beloved, now sainted mother, had come over to Liverpool to see me off. Never shall I forget that day, nor how she went with me into the cabin that was to be my home for nearly six long months. With a mother's loving hand she smoothed the little bed. She sat by my side and joined in the last hymn we should sing together before parting. We knelt down and she prayed—the last mother's prayer I was to hear before leaving for China. Then notice was given that we must separate, and we had to say good-bye, never expecting to meet on earth again.

"For my sake she restrained her feelings as much as

possible. We parted, and she went ashore giving me her blessing. I stood alone on deck, and she followed the ship as we moved toward the dock gates. As we passed through the gates and the separation really commenced, never shall I forget the cry of anguish wrung from that mother's heart. It went through me like a knife. I never knew so fully until then, what 'God so loved the world' meant. And I am quite sure my precious mother learned more of the love of God for the perishing in that one hour than in all her life before."

As difficult and emotional as that parting must have been, the trials of Hudson's around-the-world journey had just begun. It was a journey nearly doomed before the little ship even reached the open sea. For twelve stormy days the *Dumfries* beat about St. George's Channel in gale-force winds, alternately sighting Ireland and the dangerous Welsh coast. Hudson's journals tell the story:

"All day on Saturday [the 24th of September] the barometer kept falling, and as darkness came on the wind began to freshen. The sailors had a hard night of it, so the Captain did not call them aft as is his custom to read prayers on Sunday morning. At noon it was blowing hard and we took in all possible sail, leaving only just as much as would keep the ship steady. I distributed tracts among the crew and then came down to my cabin, as the increased motion was making me sick . . .

"The barometer was still falling, and the wind increased until it was a perfect hurricane. The Captain and the Mate said they had never seen a wilder sea. Between two and three in the afternoon I managed to get on deck, though the pitching made it difficult . . . The scene I shall never forget. It was grand beyond description. The sea, lashing itself into fury, was white with foam. There was a large ship astern us and a brig to our weather side. The ship gained on us, but drifted more. The waves, like hills on either side, seemed as if they might swamp us at any moment . . . but the ship bore up bravely. On account of the heavy sea we were making little or no headway, and the wind being from the west we were drifting quickly, irresistibly, toward a lee-shore.

" 'Unless God help us,' the captain said, 'There is no hope.'

"I asked how far we might be from the Welsh coast.

" 'Fifteen to sixteen miles,' was his reply. 'We can do nothing but carry all possible sail. The more we carry the less we drift. It is for our lives. God grant the timbers may bear it.'

"He then had two sails set on each mast.

"It was a fearful time. The wind was blowing terrifically, and we were tearing along at a frightful rate—one moment high in the air and the next plunging head foremost into the trough of the sea as if about to go to the bottom. The windward side of the ship was fearfully elevated, the lee side being as much depressed; indeed the sea at times poured over her lee bulwarks.

"Thus the sun set and I watched it ardently. 'Tomorrow thou wilt rise as usual,' I thought. 'But unless the Lord work miraculously on our behalf a few broken timbers will be all that is left of us and our ship' . . .

"The night was cold, the wind biting, and the seas we shipped continually, with foam and spray, wet us through and through.

"I went below, read a hymn or two, some Psalms and John 13-15, and was comforted; so much so that I fell asleep, and slept for an hour. We then looked at the barometer and found it rising. We had passed the Bardsey

Island lighthouse, between Cardigan and Carnarvon Bays (running up the Channel) and I asked the Captain whether we could clear Holyhead or not.

" 'If we make no leeway,' he replied, 'we may just do it. But if we drift, God help us!'

"And we did drift . . .

"First the Holyhead lighthouse was ahead of us, and then it was on our outside. Our fate now seemed sealed. I asked if we were sure of two more hours. The Captain could not say we were. The barometer was still rising, but too slowly to give much hope. I thought of my dear father and mother, sisters and special friends . . . and the tears would start . . . The Captain was calm and courageous, trusting in the Lord for his soul's salvation. The steward said he knew that he was nothing, but Christ was all. I felt thankful for them, but I did pray earnestly that God would have mercy on us and spare us for the sake of the unconverted crew . . . as well as for His own glory as the God who hears and answers prayer. The passage was then brought to my mind: 'Call upon me in the day of trouble; I will deliver thee, and thou shalt glorify Me': and very earnestly I pleaded the promise . . .

"Our position now was truly awful. The night was very light, the moon being unclouded, and we could just see land ahead. I went below. The barometer was improving, but the wind in no way abated. I took out my pocket-book and wrote in it my name and home-address, in case my body should be found. I also tied a few things in a hamper which I thought would float and perhaps help me or someone else to land. Then, commending my soul to God my Father, and my friends and all to His care, with one prayer that if it were possible this cup might pass from us, I went on deck.

"Satan now tempted me greatly and I had a fearful struggle. But the Lord again calmed my mind, which from that time was so stayed upon Him that I was kept in peace.

"I asked the Captain whether [life] boats could live in such a sea. He answered, 'No.' Could we not lash spars together and make some sort of raft? He said we should probably not have time.

"The water was now becoming white. Land was just ahead . . .

" 'We must try to turn her and tack,' said the Captain, 'Or all is over. The sea may sweep the deck in turning and wash everything overboard . . . but we must try.'

"This was a moment to make the stoutest heart tremble. He gave the word and we tried to turn outwardly, but in vain. This would have saved us room. He then tried the other way and with God's blessing succeeded, clearing the rocks by not more than two ships' length. Just as we did so, the wind most providentially veered two points in our favour, and we were able to beat out of the Bay.

"Had not the Lord thus helped us, all our efforts must have been in vain. Truly his mercy is unfailing."

Hudson Taylor's journal recording the events of his voyage is full of interesting experiences, occasional excitement, and even more monotony of twenty-three consecutive weeks of sailing without touching land. Much of his time was spent in his cabin, reading, studying, and preparing for his missionary ministry. But he also held more than sixty religious services for the sailors aboard the ship. The men seemed interested and some came to Hudson at times for private talk and prayer, but he was somewhat discouraged that so little permanent change resulted in their lives and that none of the men made complete commitments to Christ.

But perhaps one of the most encouraging, and most trying, experiences of the voyage occurred during days of doldrums in the South Pacific when the only progress was made between sunset and dawn when the light evening breezes would blow. Of those days Hudson wrote:

"Never is one more helpless than in a sailing ship with a total absence of wind and the presence of a strong current setting toward a dangerous coast. In a storm the ship is to some extent manageable, but becalmed one can do nothing; the Lord must do all.

"This happened notably on one occasion when we were in dangerous proximity to the north of New Guinea. Saturday night had brought us to a point some thirty miles off the land, and during the Sunday morning service which was held on deck I could not fail to see that the Captain looked troubled and frequently went over to the side of the ship. When the service was ended I learned from him the cause: a four-knot current was carrying us toward some sunken reefs, and we were already so near that it seemed improbable that we should get through the afternoon in safety. After dinner the long-boat was put out and all hands endeavoured, without success, to turn the ship's head from the shore.

"After standing together on the deck for some time in silence, the Captain said to me: 'Well, we have done everything that can be done. We can only wait the result.'

"A thought occurred to me and I replied: 'No, there is one thing we have not done yet.'

" 'What is that?' he queried.

"Four of us on board are Christians. Let us each retire to his own cabin, and in agreed prayer ask the Lord to give us immediately a breeze. He can as easily send it now as at sunset.'

Hudson Taylor's

"The Captain complied with this proposal. I went and spoke to the other two men, and after prayer with the carpenter we all four retired to wait upon God. I had a good but very brief season in prayer, and then felt so satisfied that our request was granted that I could not continue asking, and very soon went up again on deck. The first officer, a godless man, was in charge. I went over and asked him to let down the clews or corners of the mainsail, which had been drawn up in order to lessen the useless flapping of the sail against the rigging.

" 'What would be the good of that?' he answered roughly.

"I told him we had been asking a wind from God; that it was coming immediately; and we were so near the reef by this time that there was not a minute to lose.

"With an oath and a look of contempt, he said he would rather see a wind than hear of it.

"But while he was speaking I watched his eye, following it up to the royal, and there sure enough the corner of the topmost sail was beginning to tremble in the breeze.

" 'Don't you see the wind is coming? Look at the royal!' I exclaimed.

" 'No, it is only a cat's paw,' he rejoined (a mere puff of wind).

" 'Cat's paw or not,' I cried, 'Pray let down the mainsail and give us the benefit.'

"This he was not slow to do. In another minute the heavy tread of the men on deck brought up the Captain from his cabin to see what was the matter. The breeze had indeed come! In a few minutes we were ploughing our way at six or seven knots an hour through the water . . . and though the wind was sometimes unsteady we did not

Spiritual Secret

altogether lose it until after passing the Pelew Islands.

"Thus God encouraged me ere landing on China's shores to bring a variety of need to Him in prayer, and to expect that He would honour the name of the Lord Jesus and give the help each emergency required."

It was a lesson he would soon put to the test.

4

"One who is really leaning on the Beloved finds it always possible to say, 'I will fear no evil, for thou art with me.' But I am so apt, like Peter, to take my eyes off the One to be trusted and look at the winds and waves . . . Oh, for more stability!"

1854 - 1855

China seemed even more forbidding to an uninvited foreigner in 1854, when Hudson Taylor first reached its shores, than it would today. Shanghai and four other treaty ports were the only cities in which Westerners were allowed to reside. And there was not a single Protestant missionary anywhere in the interior.

The curiosity with which the Chinese people viewed foreigners was more than matched by deep feelings of suspicion and fear. Civil war was raging, and the entire country lived in chaos.

The Taiping Rebellion, which started as a populist movement for social, economic, and religious reform, and was viewed by many Westerners as the best hope for an end to the repressive Manchu dynasty, had bogged down. Lack of unity and discipline among the ranks caused the movement to disintegrate slowly into factional, destructive political strife. What many had hoped might actually result in at least a nominally Christian Chinese culture instead resulted in bitterness, violence, bloodshed, and turmoil that would continue for eleven years after Hudson Taylor's arrival in China—until the Manchu dynasty reestablished a large measure of its former power.

Years afterward, when he would himself be responsible for the guidance of many missionaries, it would be much easier to see the value of all the hard lessons learned during his early time in China. But at the time there seemed so many lessons to learn, so many hardships to experience.

Where Hudson had dreamed of traveling to the city of Nanking and soon thereafter to minister as the first evangelist in China's interior, he now found nearly insurmountable difficulties just getting established in Shanghai.

As Hudson neared the shores of China, Shanghai was in the grip of war. A renegade band of rebels known as the "Red Turbans" was in possession of the native city, near the foreign settlement. And forty to fifty thousand Imperial troops were encamped around the city. Fighting was almost continuous, and the foreign militia was frequently called upon to protect the settlement.

But Hudson Taylor knew little or none of this when he finally arrived in Shanghai on March 1, 1854. "My feelings on stepping ashore," he wrote, "I cannot attempt to describe. My heart felt as though it had no room and must burst its bonds, while tears of gratitude and thankfulness fell from my eyes."

Just as quickly the loneliness and reality of his situation sank in. Not a single person was there to meet him. Not even a stranger to shake his hand in welcome. In fact, no one in Shanghai knew he was coming. And not a soul on the entire continent knew his name. He later wrote:

"Mingled with thankfulness for deliverance from many dangers and joy at finding myself at last on Chinese soil came a vivid realisation of the great distance between me and those I loved, and that I was a stranger in a strange land.

"I had three letters of introduction, however, and counted on advice and help from one especially, to whom I had been commended by mutual friends, whom I knew well and highly valued. Of course, I inquired of him at once, only to learn that he had been buried a month or two previously, having died of fever while we were at sea.

"Saddened by these tidings, I asked the whereabouts of a missionary to whom another of my introductions was addressed, but only to meet with further disappointment. He had recently left for America. The third letter remained; but it had been given me by a comparative stranger, and I expected less from it than from the others."

Indeed, when inquiring about this third gentleman, only to be told he was no longer there, Hudson Taylor felt utterly alone. But a colleague of the third missionary invited Hudson to stay for a time on the property of the London Mission until he could be suitably settled.

Hudson soon learned of some of the challenges he would face. All consumer goods were sold at famine prices, and both the city and settlement were so crowded that suitable housing could scarcely be obtained at any price. Had it not been for the hospitality of Dr. Lockhart of the London Mission, he would have had nowhere to stay. Even so, sharp fighting was to be seen from his windows, and he was unable to walk in any direction without witnessing more horrible suffering and human misery than he'd ever imagined.

It was bitterly cold when Hudson Taylor first reached Shanghai, and since coal was selling at fifty dollars a ton, it was not possible to do much to warm the houses. Fortunately, Hudson wasn't accustomed to luxuries, and he was thankful for a shelter anywhere ashore. Yet he suffered from the penetrating chill and dampness. Soon after his arrival he wrote:

"My position is a very difficult one. Dr. Lockhart has

taken me to reside with him for the present, as houses are not to be had for love or money . . . No one can live in the city . . . They are fighting now while I write, and the house shakes with the report of cannon.

"It is so cold that I can hardly think or hold the pen. You will see from my letter to Mr. Pearse how perplexed I am. It will be four months before I can hear in reply, and the very kindness of the missionaries who have received me with open arms makes me fear to be burdensome. Jesus will guide me aright . . . I love the Chinese more than ever. Oh, to be useful among them!"

About his first Sunday in China Hudson wrote to his sister:

"I attended two services at the London Mission and in the afternoon went into the city with Mr. Wylie. You have never seen a city in a state of siege . . . God grant you never may! We walked some distance round the wall, and sad it was to see the wreck of rows upon rows of houses. Burnt down, blown down, battered to pieces—in all stages of ruin they were! And the misery of those who once occupied them and now, at this inclement season, are driven from home and shelter is terrible to think of . . .

"By the time we came to the North Gate they were fighting fiercely outside the city. One man was carried in dead, another shot through the chest, and a third whose arm I examined seemed in dreadful agony. A ball had gone clean through the arm breaking the bone in passing . . . A little farther on we met some men bringing in a small cannon they had captured, and following them were others, dragging along by their tails [their braided hair queues] five wretched prisoners. The poor fellows cried to us piteously to save them as they were hurried by, but alas, we could do nothing! They would probably be at once decapitated. It makes one's blood run cold to think of such things.

"What it means to be so far from home, at the seat of war and not be able to understand or be understood by the people was fully realised. Their utter wretchedness and misery and my inability to help them or even point them to Jesus powerfully affected me. Satan came in as a flood, but there is One who lifted up a standard against him. Jesus is here, and though unknown to the majority and uncared-for by many who might know Him, He is present and precious to His own."

There were other more personal trials as well. For the first time in his life, Hudson Taylor found himself in a position where he could hardly meet his financial obligations. He had willingly lived on next to nothing at home, to keep within his means. But in Shanghai he could not avoid expenses altogether beyond his income. Living with others who were receiving three or four times his salary, he was obligated to board as they did, and saw his small resources melt away with alarming speed.

At home in England he raised money for foreign missions; he knew what it was like to receive the hard-earned contributions of poor and working-class people for whom charitable giving was a true sacrifice. So missionary money was to him a sacred trust; to have to use it so freely caused him real distress. To make matters worse, the letters he wrote to the society asking for direction seldom received satisfactory replies. After waiting months for instructions, he might hear nothing at all in answer to his most urgent inquiries.

The society in London was far away and could in no way imagine the circumstances he faced in China. The secretaries were mostly busy men, absorbed in their own affairs, who, despite their best intentions and sincere dedication to missionary work, were simply unable to visualize a situation so different from anything they had ever known. Hudson Taylor did all he could to make matters clear to them in his regular letters, but month after month went by, and he was left in uncertainty and financial distress.

The Shanghai dollar, previously worth about fifty cents gold, was up to twice that sum and continually rising, yet it had no more purchasing value. Obliged to exceed his salary for even the barest necessities of life, he finally had to use a letter of credit provided for emergencies. Yet he could obtain no assurance from the society at home that his bills would be honored.

It was a painful situation for someone who always had been so conscientious in money matters. And it caused him many wakeful nights.

Then, in the heat of summer, his financial crisis became even more complicated. Hudson learned second-hand that the Scottish physician, who was to be his colleague, had already sailed from England with wife and children. He had received no advance instructions regarding accommodations for the family. As the weeks went by with still no word, he realized that unless he took the initiative, an entire family would be welcomed without so much as a roof over their heads. With no authorization for such an expenditure, he had to find and rent rooms of some sort for five people—in a war-torn city with little housing, at a time of exorbitant prices.

Unable even to afford a sedan chair—the proper means of transport for Europeans—he exhausted himself searching all through the city and settlement, in the blinding heat of August, for houses that were not to be had.

His friends from Shanghai suggested that the only thing to do was to buy land and build immediately.

But how could he tell them the embarrassing truth and reveal his lack of funds? He felt there had already been too much criticism in the community for the mission he represented and for its inadequate organization. If there was any hope of continuing the work in China, he felt that he had to keep his troubles to himself—at least as much as possible. And to pray.

Under these circumstances he wrote:

"One who is really leaning on the Beloved finds it always possible to say, 'I will fear no evil, for thou art with me.' But I am so apt, like Peter, to take my eyes off the One to be trusted and look at the winds and waves . . . Oh, for more stability! The reading of the Word and meditation on the promises have been increasingly precious to me of late. At first I allowed my desire to acquire the language speedily to have undue prominence and a deadening effect on my soul. But now, in the grace that passes all understanding, the Lord has again caused His face to shine upon me."

And to his sister he added:

"I have been puzzling my brains again about a house, etc., but to no effect. So I have made it a matter of prayer, and have given it entirely into the Lord's hands, and now I feel quite at peace about it. He will provide and be my guide in this and every other perplexing step."

It must have seemed almost too good to be true when, only two days after writing that letter, Hudson Taylor heard of property that could be rented. And before the month was over, he found himself in possession of a house large enough to accommodate his expected colleagues.

Five rooms upstairs and seven down seemed a

spacious residence, even if it was only a poor Chinese place—built of wood, full of enough debris "to start a pestilence" he wrote, and extremely run-down. On the positive side, it was right among the people, near the North Gate of Shanghai. So it was there that he established himself six months after he arrived in China. And even though the location was so dangerous that his Mandarin teacher did not dare to go with him, he was able to engage a Chinese Christian, an educated man, who could help him begin to learn the local dialect.

Finally Hudson felt that his missionary work in China had begun. He was living right among the people in a place of his own. And with the help of his new teacher, he conducted Christian meetings morning and evening, started a Christian day school for children, and established a dispensary where he would have as many as twenty or thirty patients a day seeking medical help.

His letters home, to family and the mission, revealed his great excitement over all these developments—as well as his continued consternation over dwindling finances. It looked as if he had no choice but to borrow more money and he still had no assurance that the mission would cover his basic expenditures. To complicate things, the location of the house that enabled him to establish a base of ministry was becoming more and more threatened by the fighting all around. In one letter to his family he wrote:

"Last Wednesday night, a fire that seemed very near awoke me at three o'clock in the morning. Dressing hastily, I climbed on to the roof to ascertain if it were coming this way. Chinese houses like these, built only of wood, burn very quickly on a windy night. It was an anxious moment, for in the darkness I fancied the burning building was only four or five doors away. Just then, as I was praying earnestly for protection, it began to rain. The wind fell, for which I was most thankful, and gradually the fire smouldered down. But it was after five before I dared go to bed again.

"While there on the roof, several bullets struck the buildings round me, and two or three seemed to fall on the tiles of my own house. At last, a heavy ball struck the ridge of the opposite roof, carrying away a lot of tiles, the fragments of which fell around me, and itself flew off obliquely. You may be sure I did not wait up there for another . . .

"The day before a ball of that size, evidently spent, struck the roof of this house, broke some tiles, and fell at the feet of my teacher's child who was standing in the doorway. Had he been half a yard further out, it might have killed him. That was at noon.

"I have never passed, as you will believe, such a trying time in my life. But it is all necessary, and I feel is being made a blessing to me. I may have to leave here suddenly . . . But whatever happens, I do not regret coming to this house, and would do it again under similar circumstances. Our Society must provide better, however, for its missionaries. This sort of thing will not do."

It grew increasingly obvious that the house he had finally found in preparation for the arrival of his colleague's family could not serve its intended purpose. It was far too dangerous for a family. So by the end of October, as conditions worsened, he wrote the secretaries:

"There is a great deal of firing going on here now, so much so that . . . I am seldom able to get half a night's sleep. What Dr. Parker and his family are to do, I do not know. Their coming here as things are now is out of the question. This constant anxiety for them as well as myself, together with another still more trying [issue] (the expense I am unable to avoid) is by no means a desirable addition to the difficulties of language and climate . . .

"We have heard nothing of the *Swiftsure*, but she is hardly due as yet. I shall be thankful when Dr. Parker is here and we are able to consult together about the future. You will find this a much more expensive Mission, I fear, than was anticipated . . . I shall have to draw again this month, and with all possible economy cannot alter the high rate of prices. The total expense of my first year will be little under two hundred pounds, and even so I feel confident that there is no other missionary in Shanghai who will not have cost considerably more . . ."

Indeed, Hudson Taylor had become the subject of much gossip in the foreign community of Shanghai. Not only had he chosen to live outside the foreign settlement and among the Chinese, he did little socializing among other Westerners and even his clothing was looking worn and tattered.

When at last the house next door to Hudson's was set on fire in an attempt to drive him out, he felt he had no choice but to return to the foreign settlement and his friends at the London Mission. And it was at that time that a small home on the London Missionary Society property became available for rent. It had belonged to his closest friends in China, a missionary couple named Burdon. Mrs. Burdon had died shortly after giving birth and Mr. Burdon had left with his baby daughter. Their house was suddenly for rent. Since the arrival of the Parkers was expected daily, and though it left him with only three dollars, Hudson rented the house on his own authority. Two days later, his long-awaited colleagues, the Parkers, arrived with two young children plus an infant born at sea.

To make matters worse, Dr. Parker, after the expenses of the voyage, landed in Shanghai with only a few dollars. He was expecting a letter of credit from the society to have already arrived. But it hadn't. And it didn't. In fact, subsequent letters from the home office of the society didn't even mention the expected money.

Hudson was able to ease the financial strain by subleasing half the house to an American missionary family. But that left only three rooms for the Parkers, their three young children, and himself.

Dr. Parker went regularly with Hudson to evangelize in the city and the surrounding villages. At home the men devoted hours every day to the study of Chinese. But the lack of privacy and the lack of provisions proved both trying and irritating.

Hudson, who for months had been exceedingly patient and understanding about his own financial straits, wrote an indignant letter to the society on behalf of the Parkers in which he said:

"I trust you will not deem it unkind or disrespectful of me to write thus. For though I feel these things and feel them keenly, were it not for the sake of others and the good of the Society I would pass over them in silence. To do this, however, would be unfaithfulness on my part. For not only is it morally wrong and thoughtless in the extreme to act as the Society has acted towards Dr. Parker, but you must surely see that men who can quadruple their salary by professional practise, or double it by taking a clerk's berth will not be likely, if they find themselves totally unprovided for, to continue in the service of the Society. I do not make these remarks with respect to Dr. Parker, who seems thoroughly devoted to the work and by his spirit has encouraged me not a little. But they are true none the less.

And I may add that a vacant post at 200 pounds a year, the whole duties of which would not occupy two hours in the evening, did look inviting to me at a time when I had been obliged to incur a responsibility of 120 pounds for rent, and a Resolution upon my last letter to the Committee informed me that missionaries drawing more than was authorised would not have their bills honoured by the Society.

"Dr. Parker arrived on Monday, a week ago today, calling forth true gratitude to God for deliverance from the many dangers that had beset their path. Of course, he found our half of the house nearly empty, as my few things did not go far in furnishing. The [other] missionaries, when they discovered the lack of preparation, blamed me very much. Could I tell them that having paid nearly 20 pounds for rent I had only three dollars left . . . a sum not sufficient to purchase provisions for a week at the present high rate of prices?

"The weather is now exceedingly cold, and not having been led to expect it the Parkers needed an immediate supply of warm clothing. Beds and other articles of furniture were also necessary, as well as food and firing, all of which run into a considerable sum. Though he has said little, I am sure Dr. Parker has felt it keenly. I do trust that you will avoid such occurrences in future, that your missionaries will be spared unnecessary suffering."

Throughout his first difficult months in China, made so much more difficult by the lack of consideration and the bureaucratic ineptitude within his mission, Hudson avoided a spirit of bitterness. In fact, since several of the secretaries had become close friends and had shared such meaningful spiritual fellowship with him before he'd left England, Hudson actually missed them and longed for their company. But he also longed for some way to effectively communicate the needs of missionaries to supporters back home who couldn't imagine their circumstances.

Those long days of frustration taught him much about how a mission needed to be run. And as seen in a letter to his sister Amelia, he tried to find the good in a bad situation:

"You ask how I get over my troubles. This is the way . . . I take them to the Lord. Since writing the above, I have been reading my evening portion—Psalms 72 to 74. Read them and see how applicable they are. I don't know how it is, but I can seldom read scripture now without tears of joy and gratitude . . .

"I see that to be as I am and have been since my arrival has really been more conducive to improvement and progress than any other position would have been, though in many respects it has been painful and far from what I should myself have chosen. Oh, for more implicit reliance on the wisdom and love of God!"

He would soon need it. Because the young missionary's troubles were going to get worse.

5

"At the lowest computation five or six
hundred persons must have been present . . .
As they quieted down, I addressed them at
the top of my voice . . . It was most
encouraging to hear one and another call
out . . . 'puh-tso, puh-tso,' 'not wrong, not
wrong,' as they frequently did when
something said met with their approval."

1855

Perhaps the most surprising and impressive aspect of Hudson Taylor's first two years in China was the way he threw himself into pioneer missionary travel. Here he was alone, a mere boy barely into his twenties, in a country unimaginably different from home, still learning the language and with virtually no financial resources. A violent civil war raged all around, often in sight of his residence. And because foreigners had at one time or another supported both sides in the ongoing revolution, Westerners were hated by many Chinese and universally viewed with suspicion. Yet despite these circumstances, Hudson Taylor embarked on no less than ten missionary journeys in those first two years— sometimes in company with another missionary, but several times traveling by himself. Each trip was a tribute to his spiritual courage and his physical endurance.

North, south, and west of Shanghai stretched a populous region reachable through an intricate network of seemingly endless waterways. Junks, small Chinese sailing vessels, were plentiful. They afforded shelter of a sort at night, as well as transportation by day. And boat travelers didn't have to depend on the inconvenient, dangerous, and primitive Chinese inns.

Simple cooking arrangements aboard the junks supplied food for the boatsman's family, the crew, and "guests." Conditions were crude: the beds were just wooden boards, and the tiny windows were often at the level of the floor. But passengers could lie down or sit on their bedding when it was not possible to stand upright. Though travel was slow and dependent on tides and weather, millions of people were accessible on shore in city after city, town after town. New villages were never out of sight as the junks sailed slowly along. Most of them had never been visited by a foreigner; even fewer had heard the Christian gospel.

This was what drew Hudson Taylor, who longed to follow Jesus' example by preaching throughout the countryside. He felt the same "must" Jesus had expressed centuries before: "I must work the works of him that sent me"; "I must preach the kingdom of God to other cities also"; "Other sheep I have, . . . them also I must bring." It was not enough to minister on the crowded streets of Shanghai. Others were already doing that to some extent. His heart was burdened with a sense of responsibility for those beyond—those who had never ever heard the gospel of Christ, who would never hear unless an outside messenger brought them the message. So nothing held him back. Not winter cold or summer heat or deadly disease. Hudson was not even daunted by the perils of war, which not only endangered the lives of any European, but could, at any time, cut him off from return to the comparative safety of the foreign settlement in Shanghai.

Before Dr. Parker arrived, and in the time right afterward, foreigners made many excursions to places within ten or fifteen miles of Shanghai. On similar day trips during the first three months the new colleagues were together, Taylor and Parker distributed eighteen hundred New Testaments and Scripture portions in addition to two thousand explanatory books and tracts. These were carefully placed only with those who could read. And since the majority of the people were illiterate, the message of the books was carefully explained to the constantly changing crowds.

Then, beginning in winter, the missionary team took four extended journeys from January to March, in spite of zero-degree weather. It seemed that everywhere they stepped ashore, the two young missionaries automatically drew a crowd—as much to gawk at the strange-looking men in their even stranger-looking Western clothes as to listen to their teachings. On more than one occasion Taylor and Parker were threatened by hostile crowds. They were once taken captive by a band of militia who wanted to kill them; but when the local magistrate heard their message, he ordered that they be freed and given safe conduct to travel and preach in his city.

The welcome at most places was far more positive. Initial curiosity at the sight of the foreigners was quickly replaced by genuine interest and friendliness. And there was usually such an open response to their preaching that they had no trouble giving away thousands more Chinese New Testaments and supplemental tracts and books to those who wanted to learn more about this Jesus they talked about.

So the young missionaries didn't know what to make of the strange response they received on a March trip to Kia-ting, a city north and west of Shanghai up Soo-Chow Creek. As Dr. Parker reported: "Even grown men took refuge in their houses as we drew near, hastily shutting the doors; to which, however, they crowded to look after us as soon as we had passed."

Realizing that the people of this city not only had never seen foreigners but had heard fearful tales about

Hudson Taylor's

them, the two missionaries walked about openly so they could be easily seen. They told anyone who would listen that they were physicians who would gladly, and free of charge, examine and treat patients the next day. Word quickly spread that these men were "doers of good deeds," and a still-fearful crowd began to follow them about the city at a distance. Before long the crowd had grown so large that shop-fronts were in danger and some merchandise displayed outside was getting trampled. The missionaries had no choice but to seek out more open sections of the city so as not to annoy the shopkeepers and other business people.

Dr. Parker wrote about the events of the next morning:

"Long before breakfast the banks of the river were crowded with persons desiring medical aid . . . After working hard until 3 p.m., finding we could not possibly see them all, Mr. Taylor selected the more urgent cases and brought them on board the boat. No sooner were those attended to than we were taken to see patients in their own homes who were unable to come to us, and were much gratified to find that we had access to and were welcomed in some of the very houses the doors of which had been shut against us the day before."

From that day on, they met nothing but friendliness in that city. And when they preached a parting message in a temple near the city's west gate, many people asked them to stay. But the missionaries journeyed on.

Everywhere they went people wanted to know more. Hudson was overwhelmed and challenged by the opportunity and the need they witnessed. From temple-crowned hilltops and the heights of ancient pagodas, he would look down upon cities, towns, and villages where the homes of millions of people were in sight—men, women, and children who had never heard the name of the One he had come to tell them about. There was so much to be done. So many people to reach.

No sooner would one journey be completed than he would begin preparing for the next. In April, on a journey he took with Mr. Burdon, his missionary friend whose wife had died the year before, he found the city of Tsung-ming, on an island in the Yangtze River, particularly receptive. They were invited to speak in four of the city's largest temples, much like the missionaries of the New Testament. And in the temple of the city-god, Hudson set up a temporary clinic in a side room to care for patients while Burdon kept the crowd occupied with books and preaching in the open courtyard.

Only when his friend's voice gave out did Hudson quit doctoring and take over the preaching. Since he wasn't as tall as his friend, he climbed atop one of the temple's large brass incense vases and began to address the crowd. He wrote about the experience:

"At the lowest computation five or six hundred persons must have been present, and I do not think it would be over the mark to say a thousand. As they quieted down, I addressed them at the top of my voice, and a more orderly, attentive audience in the open air one could not wish to see. It was most encouraging to hear one and another call out . . . 'puh-tso, puh-tso,' 'not wrong, not wrong,' as they frequently did when something said met with their approval."

Heartening response during each trip made Hudson all the more excited about the next. So he continued his inland trips during the sweltering months of May, June, August, and September. Out among the crowds all day, and in boats that had to be closed at night because of river thieves, there was little relief from the distressing heat. Yet even that didn't slow his pace. During May alone he traveled for twenty-five days during which he preached in fifty-eight different cities, fifty-one of which had never been visited by a Protestant missionary.

During this time, the civil war reached a major turning point as Shanghai finally fell before the Imperial government forces. Hudson Taylor was traveling at the time with older missionaries toward Soochow Lake. They had only been gone a few days when, looking back toward Shanghai from the top of a hill, they saw so much smoke they knew it could mean just one thing—Shanghai was in flames!

Worried for the safety of the families and friends they'd left behind in the foreign settlement, the group set out at once to return to the city. Even before they reached Shanghai itself, their fears were confirmed by fleeing rebels who begged for their protection. But there was nothing Hudson or his friends could do to help them. In fact, the men were quickly captured by Imperial forces and beheaded before the missionaries' eyes.

Hurrying on toward the foreign settlement with growing apprehension, they witnessed more evidence of terrible destruction wherever they turned. But upon finally reaching the walls of the foreign settlement itself they were relieved to find it just as they had left it. Perhaps because the Imperialist troops were satiated by the slaughter they had inflicted on the rebels and the native population of Shanghai, they were too exultant over their conquest to pay much attention to the foreigners. Hudson Taylor wrote home in his report:

"Shanghai is now in peace, but it is like the peace of death. Two thousand people at the very least have perished, and the tortures some of the victims have undergone cannot be exceeded by the worst barbarities of the Inquisition. The city is little more than a mass of ruins, and many of the wretched objects who survive are piteous to behold."

But the worst of the war danger was over. Hudson Taylor and his colleagues now gave themselves to caring for the spiritual and physical needs of Shanghai's survivors, while they waited anxiously for the reply of their society to their suggestions for more settled work. Having seen the opportunities and the needs firsthand, Hudson and the Parkers prayed, asking God for a strategy that would make them most useful in China.

They concluded that their mission needed to purchase land in Shanghai. On that land they should build medical facilities for Dr. Parker to establish a practice and also a permanent base from which they could launch more itinerant evangelism ventures inland. So after much discussion and prayer, they wrote to the secretaries, requesting the necessary money. With the fall of Shanghai to the Imperialists, the timing became even more crucial. Now that the siege had ended and rebuilding had begun, the local economy was set to take off. Thousands of Chinese opportunists began pouring into the city from the surrounding region. Their presence, plus a new influx of like-minded foreigners, sent prices soaring once again.

Months passed as the missionaries waited for word on their request. The heat of the summer, meanwhile, was overpowering in their crowded quarters. A brief visit to the great coastal city of Ning-po over a hundred miles to the south opened up an appealing alternative to their uncertain situation in Shanghai. Several missionary groups in that city, sensing the need for a hospital to supplement their otherwise effective ministries, proposed that Dr. Parker move to that city to establish a medical work. The different agencies represented there even pledged the financial support needed for Dr. Parker to get started in Ning-po.

Still Hudson and the Parkers awaited word on their proposal for establishing a permanent mission headquarters in Shanghai. The need for an answer became even more crucial as they received notice that the house they were sharing with another family would be needed shortly—for members of the mission to which it belonged. And still there were no other rooms for rent anywhere in the settlement or the city.

Finally the answer came. But what a discouraging answer it was. The committee had made a firm decision; they said their organization was philosophically opposed to spending money on building in the ports because they saw their mission and that of their workers to be the evangelism of the interior. They didn't want to be hampered by getting too rooted in the port cities.

While the decision must have seemed a sound one from where the secretaries sat on the other side of the world, and while their missionaries in China shared the vision for carrying the gospel into the interior, the decision did nothing to solve the immediate problem of where they were to live until the society's mission was feasible.

Deeply disappointed by the response, Dr. and Mrs. Parker decided to accept the offer of a new medical work in Ning-po. While Hudson supported his friends' decision, he was left in even more uncertainty. His colleagues were leaving, his home was gone, and with no accommodations to be found even in the native city, how was he to remain in Shanghai to continue his work?

In the midst of his discouragement, Hudson began to

Spiritual Secret   *63*

develop an idea. If he could not get a home on shore, why not take to the boats as many Chinese did and live on the water? That would coincide nicely with something else he'd been thinking about; he had made up his mind that the best way to live among and minister to the Chinese was to adopt the Chinese customs of dress.

Yes, he could see how it would work. He would take his few belongings to Ning-po, when he went to escort the Parkers, and would return to a new life in which he would identify himself completely with the Chinese people to whom he had dedicated his life.

Hudson realized this was a momentous decision. Adopting Chinese dress would mean shaving the front part of his head and letting the hair grow long in back to be braided into a regulation queue. No missionaries or any other foreigners conformed to such a custom. For an occasional journey a Chinese gown might be worn over ordinary Western clothing, but to give up European clothing altogether in favor of Chinese dress would be another matter entirely. He would not only be criticized, his decision would probably result in total rejection.

But it was access to the people that he desired. And his recent journey 200 miles up the Yangtze in May had convinced Hudson that much more could be accomplished by itinerant evangelism than many had supposed. But the weariness and strain of the journey had been largely due to the fact that he was wearing European clothing, a most outlandish costume to those who had never seen it before! Attention was continually distracted from his message by his appearance, which to his hearers was as undignified as it was comical. He was sure it would have been much easier if he'd only been more suitably attired from the Chinese point of view. And if it furthered his relationship with his Chinese listeners, he decided that he didn't care what the foreign community thought. So he ordered a Chinese outfit made for his journey to Ning-po with the Parkers and readied himself for his personal, cross-cultural transformation.

It was an August evening when Hudson went down to the river to engage the junk that was to take the Parkers on the first stage of their journey. On the way a Chinese stranger approached him, asking to his surprise if he was seeking a house for rent. Would a small one do, and in the Chinese city? Near the South Gate there was such a house, but its builder had not quite finished construction when he had run short of money. He couldn't complete the work. But if the house suited Hudson, no deposit would be asked, and it could probably be had for an advance of six months' rent.

As if in a wonderful dream, Hudson Taylor followed his guide to the southern part of the city, and there found a small, compact house, perfectly new and clean, with two rooms upstairs, two on the ground floor, and a fifth across the courtyard for servants. Just the arrangement he needed for his work and in the locality he would have chosen. This last-minute answer to prayer seemed clear guidance from God that Hudson's work in Shanghai was not yet over.

That same night he visited a Chinese barber for the beginning of his transformation from European to Chinese fashion. And the next morning he appeared for the first time in public dressed as a Chinese "teacher"—a man of the scholarly class. It was in his new costume that he accompanied the Parkers to their new home in Ning-po and about which he wrote this amusing letter to his sister on August 28, 1855:

"My Dear Amelia—By way of surprise I mean to

write you a letter—for I know you have never received one before from a man with a long tail and shaven head! But lest your head should be bewildered with conjecture, I had better tell you at once that on Thursday last at 11 p.m. I resigned my locks to the barber, dyed my hair a good black, and in the morning had a proper queue plaited in with my own, and a quantity of heavy silk to lengthen it out according to Chinese custom. Then, in Chinese dress, I set out with Dr. Parker, accompanying him about a hundred miles on his way to Ning-po. This journey we made an occasion for evangelistic work, and now that I am returning alone I hope to have even better facilities for book-distribution and preaching.

"But I have not commenced the recital of my tribulations, and as there is some doubt as to whether they will all go into a single letter, the sooner I begin the better.

"First then, it is a very sore thing to have one's head shaved for the first time, especially if the skin is irritable with prickly heat. And I can assure you that the subsequent application of hair dye for five or six hours, (Litharge 1 part; quick lime, freshly slaked, 3 parts; water enough to make a cream) does not do much to soothe the irritation. But when it comes to combing out the remaining hair which has been allowed to grow longer than usual, the climax is reached! But there are no gains without pain, and certainly if suffering for the thing makes it dearer, I shall regard my queue when I attain one with no small amount of pride and affection.

"Secondly, when you proceed to your toilet, you no longer wonder that many Chinese in the employ of Europeans wear foreign shoes and stockings as soon as they can get them. For native socks are made of calico and of course are not elastic . . . and average toes decidedly object to be squeezed out of shape, nor do one's heels appreciate their low position in perfectly flat-soled shoes. Next come the breeches—but oh, what unheard-of garments! Mine are two feet too wide for round the waist, which amplitude is laid in a fold in front, and kept in place by a strong girdle. The legs are short, not coming much below the knee, and wide in proportion with the waist measurement. Tucked into the long, white socks, they have a bloomer-like fullness capable, as Dr. Parker remarked, of storing a fortnight's provisions! No shirt is worn. But a white, washing-jacket, with sleeves as wide as ladies affected 20 years ago, supplies its place. And over all goes a heavy silk gown of some rich or delicate colour, with sleeves equally wide and reaching 12 or 15 inches beyond the tips of one's fingers—folded back of course when the hands are in use. Unfortunately no cap or hat is used at this season of the year, except on state occasions, which is trying as the sun is awfully hot.

"Wednesday, August 29—I do not know, dear Amelia, whether you are weary of these details. But I have no time for more upon the subject, so will dismiss it with only a mention of the shampooing I got from the barber the other day. I thought I had better go in for it as part of the proceedings, for I might be in difficulty some day if found to be uninitiated. So I bore with an outrageous tickling as long as I could, and then the beating commenced! And my back was really sore in places before it was over. On the next occasion, however, I stood it better, and I hope to acquit myself creditably in time with regard to this phase of the barber's art.

"While still with Dr. Parker on the way to Hang-chow Bay I was frequently recognised as a foreigner, because of having to speak to him in English, but today in going about

Hai-yen City no one even guessed that such a being was near. It was not until I began to distribute books and see patients that I became known. Then of course, my men were asked where I came from, and the news soon spread. Dressed in this way one is not so much respected at first sight as one might be in foreign clothing. But a little medical work soon puts that all right, and it is evidently to be one's chief help for the interior. Women and children, it seems to me, manifest more readiness to come for medical aid now than they did before . . . and in this way too, I think the native costume will be of service."

It was the "interior" that more and more filled his thoughts and his prayers—even as he settled into his new home in Shanghai. Everything he did was in preparation for that calling. And in that preparation he found great encouragement. In October he wrote:

"Dr. Parker is in Ning-po but I am not alone. I have such a sensible presence of God with me as I never before experienced, and such drawings to prayer and watchfulness as are very blessed and necessary."

So it was with renewed spirits that, despite the comfort of a new place of his own and numerous opportunities all around him in Shanghai, Hudson Taylor set out once again for the regions beyond. This time he went alone and dressed like the Chinese people themselves. And the advantages of his new strategy became quickly apparent.

His destination on this journey was the great island and city of Tsung-ming which had a population of more than a million people without a single Protestant missionary. Hudson had been well received months before on his visit to Tsung-ming with his friend Burdon, but the reception he received this time amazed him.

At his first landing place, the people simply would not hear of his leaving. Those who had seen foreigners before had never seen one dressed in Chinese custom. This teacher didn't seem at all like an outsider. His medicine chest attracted them as much as his preaching. So when they learned that he would need an upstairs room, because of the dampness of the area, they said:

"Let him live in the temple, if no other upper storey can be found."

But a householder stepped forward to say that he had an empty attic apartment. So within three days of his arrival in Tsung-ming, Hudson Taylor found himself in possession of his first home in "inland China." After all his difficulties getting established in Shanghai, this was exciting reassurance for the young missionary. Almost as exciting as the response of the people in Tsung-ming.

Neighbors dropped in every day to the meetings, and the stream of visitors and patients seemed unceasing. Six weeks of this encouraging work, while it wakened some opposition on the part of the Chinese medical fraternity, resulted in a group of regular Chinese listeners who earnestly wanted to learn about Christianity. One of these was a blacksmith named Chang, and another a successful businessman "whose heart," Hudson wrote, "the Lord opened." Hudson's own first Chinese convert, Kwei-hwa (from Shanghai), and another Christian helper were with him. So when the missionary had to return to Shanghai for supplies, the little group of new believers and seekers was still well cared for.

But the heartening success in Tsung-ming turned to bitter disappointment during one of his trips back to Shanghai, where he found an official summons waiting for him. He was to report to the British consulate at once.

Unknown to Hudson, a small group of Chinese doctors and druggists in Tsung-ming had pulled some strings. They'd bribed a local official to carry to the authorities their complaints about this "foreign doctor" who was interfering with their work by accepting no payment for his medical practice. The Chinese official did complain to the British authorities, and the Consul called Hudson in to remind him that the British treaty with China only provided for residence in the port. And if he attempted to settle elsewhere he would be subject to a fine of five hundred dollars. Hudson pleaded his case, pointing out that French priests were living in Tsung-ming, protected by a supplemental treaty which stipulated that any immunities granted to other nations should also apply to the British. But the Consul said that he didn't have the authority to make that ruling; any appeal would need to go to his superiors. In the meantime, Hudson was ordered out of Tsung-ming and instructed not to transgress the treaty in the future.

So it looked as if he would have to give up the successful new ministry that had excited and encouraged him so. And he'd also have to give up that "first home in the interior" that had seemed like such a clear sign of God's direction and blessing on his work.

6

"Those happy months were an unspeakable joy and comfort to me. Never had I such a spiritual father as Mr. Burns; never did I know such holy, happy [friendship]."

1855 - 1856

It was a frustrated, heartbroken letter Hudson Taylor wrote home that evening. Those young inquirers in Tsung-ming—Chang, Sung, and the others—what was to become of them? Weren't they now his own children in the faith? How could he leave them with no help and so little Christian knowledge? He inquired in his letter to the secretaries about his responsibilities and limitations:

"Forbidden to reside on the island and finding that even travelling into the country and remaining for a short time is an infringement of the Treaty which may be visited by a fine of 500 dollars, I have thought it best to write privately and enquire whether, in case I should be fined . . . the Society should be responsible for the sum? Also whether, if circumstances should make it possible for me to go to the interior, giving up all claim to Consular protection, you would approve my doing so? Should I be left free to follow this course? Or would the Society object to one of their missionaries adopting such a position?

"Although the attempt to rent a house and reside in Tsung-ming has met with failure, we must be very thankful for what has been accomplished. I have every reason to hope that three of those who profess to believe in the Lord Jesus are sincere, and if so the results will last to all eternity . . . At the same time it makes it all the harder to give up the work.

". . . pray for me. I do not want on the one hand to flee

from danger, nor on the other to court troubles, or from lack of patience to hinder future usefulness . . ."

Hudson determined to challenge the Consul's ruling by taking the matter before the British minister who was scheduled to arrive in Shanghai within weeks. But in the meantime there was nothing to do but take his sad leave from Tsung-ming.

"My heart will be truly sorrowful when I can no longer join you in the meetings," said the Chinese blacksmith the last evening the little group was together.

"But you will worship in your own home," Hudson told him. "Still shut your shop on Sunday, for God is here whether I am or not. Get some one to read for you, and gather your neighbors in to hear the Gospel."

"I know but very little," Sung added, "and when I read I by no means understand all the characters. My heart is grieved because you have to leave us; but I do thank God that He ever sent you to this place. My sins, once so heavy, are all laid on Jesus, and He daily gives me joy and peace."

Hudson returned to Shanghai and the even more disheartening news that the British minister was delayed. Any hope for appeal would have to be put off. In his discouragement, Hudson wrote his parents:

"Pray for me. I need more grace, and live far below my privileges. Oh to feel more as . . . the Lord Jesus Christ did when he said, 'I lay down my life for my sheep.' I do not want to be as a hireling who flees when the wolf is near, nor would I lightly run into danger when much may be accomplished in safety. I want to know the Lord's will and to have grace to do it, even if it results in expatriation. Pray for me, that I may be a follower of Christ not in word only, but in deed and truth."

It was at this low point in his life that prayers for

encouragement (both Hudson's prayers and the prayers of those who cared about him) were answered in a most unexpected way. William Burns, a preacher and evangelist, who had become a household name in Scotland during that country's great revival in 1839, had also felt a call to evangelize the interior of China. In an attempt to reach the Taiping rebel capital of Nanking, he actually journeyed far up the Yangtze River before he was turned back. So it was that he ended up in Shanghai where he met the young Hudson Taylor who was still stinging from his own recent failure.

Despite the disparity in age, the two men discovered they were kindred spirits. And like those New Testament missionaries, Paul and Timothy, they were drawn together in friendship as well as ministry.

Soon their two boats began traveling together over the network of waterways leading inland from Shanghai. The older missionary had developed a strategy of his own for such work; and Hudson gladly adopted it. Choosing an important trade center, they might remain two or three weeks in one place. Every morning they set out early with a definite plan, sometimes going to the outskirts of a city in which foreigners had rarely been seen. From a city's perimeter they would work their way slowly into the more crowded quarters. So they would give several days to preaching in the suburbs, gradually approaching the thronging streets and markets by which time they were familiar figures and could pass without attracting a rowdy, curious crowd that would arouse the shopkeepers' tempers or endanger their wares. They would also visit temples, schools, and tea shops, returning regularly to the best places for preaching. Announcing at each meeting when they would be there again, they were encouraged to see many of the same faces again and again. And those interested hearers could be invited to the boats for further conversation.

Just as Hudson learned from his older friend, William Burns also learned from him. As time went on, the Scottish evangelist could not fail to notice that Hudson Taylor, though so much younger and less experienced, had the more attentive hearers wherever they journeyed. Hudson was even asked into private houses while he himself was often requested to wait outside. The riffraff of the crowd always seemed to gather round the preacher in foreign dress, while those who wished to hear undisturbed followed his less noticeable young friend. Mr. Burns wrote about his experiences with Hudson in this letter, dated January 26, 1856:

"It is now forty-one days since I left Shanghai on this last occasion. An excellent young English missionary, Mr. Taylor of the Chinese Evangelisation Society, has been my companion . . . and we have experienced much mercy, and on some occasions considerable help in our work.

"I must once more tell the story I have had to tell more than once already, how four weeks ago, on the 29th of December, I put on Chinese dress which I am now wearing. Mr. Taylor had made this change a few months before, and I found that he was in consequence so much less incommoded in preaching, etc., by the crowd, that I concluded that it was my duty to follow his example . . .

"We have a large, very large field of labour in this region, though it might be difficult in the meantime for one to establish himself in any one particular place. The people listen with attention but we need the power from on high to convince and convert. Is there any spirit of prayer on our behalf among God's people in Kilsyth? Or is there any effort to seek the Spirit? How great the need is, and how great the arguments and motives for prayer in this case! The harvest here is indeed great, and the labourers are few and imperfectly fitted, without much grace, for such a work. And yet, grace can make a few feeble instruments the means of accomplishing great things—things greater even than we can conceive."

Daily prayer and Bible study were the foundation and the cornerstone of William Burns's life. His biographer wrote:

"He was mighty in the Scriptures and his greatest power in preaching was the way in which he used 'the sword of the Spirit' upon men's consciences and hearts . . . Sometimes one might have thought, in listening to his solemn appeals, that one was hearing a new chapter in the Bible when first spoken by a living prophet . . . His whole life was literally a life of prayer, and his ministry a series of battles fought at the mercy-seat . . . In digging in the field of the Word, he threw up now and then great nuggets which formed part of one's spiritual wealth ever after."

A cultured, genial, and witty man who enjoyed singing, William Burns proved not only to be a powerful spiritual role model in Hudson Taylor's life, he was a wonderfully lively companion and friend. He loved to tell stories and was happy to share the wisdom of his long years of experience with his young friend. As a result, Hudson's time spent with William Burns was as instructive as any university degree—and far more practical. Because William Burns lived out before him, right there in China, the reality of all Hudson needed to be and know.

"If a man have Christ in his heart," William Burns would say, "heaven before his eyes, and only as much of temporal blessing as is just needful to carry him safely through life, then pain and sorrow have little to shoot at . . . To be in Union with Him Who is Shepherd of Israel, to walk very near Him Who is both sun and shield, comprehends all a poor sinner requires to make him happy between this and heaven."

So it was that the two men worked together for seven long, happy months. It was during this time, as they continued their travels around the Shanghai region, that a Captain Bowers, a Christian ship's captain, told them about the great need to establish a mission in the city of Swatow. Even as the captain talked, Hudson began to feel the calling of God to that great southern port to which no missionaries had ever gone. But he resisted the feeling for some time because he dreaded the thought of parting from his friend.

Finally the evening came when he could resist his sense of calling no longer. He later wrote about the occasion:

"I asked Mr. Burns to come to the little house that was still my headquarters, and there with many tears I told him how the Lord had been leading me, and how rebellious I had been, and unwilling to leave him for this new sphere. He listened with a strange look of surprise and pleasure rather than of pain, and replied that he had determined that very night to tell me that he had heard the Lord's call to Swatow, and that his one regret had been the severance of our happy fellowship."

Arriving in Swatow, the two missionaries could find only a single room to rent over an incense shop in a crowded quarter of the city. When Captain Bowers visited them soon afterwards, he described their situation in a letter to a mutual friend back home:

"Seeking out his wretched lodging in Swatow

amongst the degraded of every class, I remarked, 'Surely, Mr. Burns, you might find a better place to live.' He laughingly told me that he was more content in the midst of this people than he would be at home surrounded by every comfort. He said his expenses amounted to ten dollars a month. 'Mr. Burns,' I exclaimed, 'That would not keep me in cigars!' He said it was sufficient for him."

To William Burns and Hudson Taylor, ten dollars a month for a single room, even a room they had to enter through an opening in the floor, seemed like a bargain. But if it hadn't been for their inconspicuous Chinese dress, it is doubtful that they could have survived, let alone preach and make the friendships they did in that violent, hostile city.

Europeans were suspect in Swatow because of the foreign involvement in the drug and slavery trade which plagued this corrupt city and about which Hudson wrote his family:

"About two hundred boxes of opium are imported monthly. Each box contains forty balls of about four pounds in weight. Thus not less than thirty-two thousand pounds weight of opium enter China every month at this port alone, the cost of which is about a quarter of a million sterling. After this you will not be surprised to learn that the people are wretchedly poor, ignorant, and vicious.

"A cruel slave trade also is carried on under the name of the 'coolie traffic'. The men are engaged (nominally) for a certain term of years, but few live to return. A bounty is paid them, and they are told they are going to make their fortunes, or they are entrapped by worse means. Once on the ship the agent receives so much a head for the poor fellows who soon find themselves in captivity of the most horrible kind. Some jump overboard in their efforts to escape, but they are generally retaken and flogged. Some ships carry a thousand and others three or four hundred, and very many die before reaching their destination— Cuba, Havana, and Calla . . . Of one ship with several hundreds on board, I heard the surgeon say that not more than two-thirds would survive the voyage. Poor people!"

In a later letter to his sister he wrote more about the conditions he saw around him:

"If ever there were a place needing the blessings of the Gospel, it is certainly this place. Men are sunk so low as to have lost all sense of shame . . . lower even than the beasts that perish. The official classes are as bad as the rest, and instead of restraining evil are governed themselves by opium and love of money. And if it be possible to live worse lives than the heathen, then the sailors and others [foreigners] who frequent Double Island [do so].

"Sin does indeed reign here, and, as always, those most to be pitied and whose case seems most hopeless are the women. However low men sink in heathen lands, women sink lower. Looked upon as hardly having any soul, girls are sold here for wives or slaves, and are left entirely without education. Married women and families are not numerous in proportion to the population, but the number of unfortunate women is great. I say unfortunate advisedly, for they are bought and brought up for this very purpose. They are the absolute property of their owners, and have no escape from that which many of them abhor. Only a few nights ago I was distressed by heart-rending screams from two female voices, and, on enquiring, was told that they were most likely newly bought women in a house near by, who were being tortured into submission. 'And that,' added my informant, 'is very common here.' The cries went on for about two hours. Poor things!

"This is hardly a fit subject to write to you about, but, unless you know, how can you pity and pray for them? English women little realise all they owe to the Gospel . . ."

It was in such a setting that Hudson Taylor and William Burns not only lived and survived, but saw such heartening response to their message and made so many friends that they were able, after only four months, to rent an entire house that would serve as the headquarters of their growing ministry. It was at this point that the older missionary convinced Hudson to return to Shanghai for his medical supplies in order that they could open a hospital as part of their work in Swatow.

Hudson went, but only reluctantly. He hated to leave the older man alone to face the oppressive heat (and accompanying diseases) of summer as much as he dreaded the temporary end of the companionship that had come to mean so much to him.

He recalled the time later saying:

"Those happy months were an unspeakable joy and comfort to me. Never had I such a spiritual father as Mr. Burns; never did I know such holy, happy [friendship]. His love for the Word was delightful, and his holy reverential life and constant communing with God made fellowship with him to satisfy the deep cravings of my heart."

But Hudson did indeed sail for Shanghai, where he made the disheartening discovery that all his medical supplies had been destroyed by fire. And before he could replace them and return to Swatow, he received the even more distressing news that William Burns had been arrested by the corrupt Chinese authorities in Swatow and sent, under escort, on a harsh, thirty-one-day journey to Canton. Hudson himself was forbidden to return to Swatow.

Suddenly the path that had seemed so clear before him was again blocked. And yet it was this latest obstacle in his life's journey that sent him on a detour that he would never once regret.

7

"How blessedly He did lead me I can never, never tell. It was like a continuation of some of my earlier experiences at home. My faith was not untried . . . But oh! I was learning to know Him. I would not even then have missed the trial. He became so near, so real, so intimate!"

1856 - 1858

Over the political horizon, storm clouds had been gathering for many months. Now the very mail that brought tidings of William Burns's arrest told also of the outbreak of hostilities between England and China. Hudson had traveled to see Dr. Parker in Ning-po in hopes that he might have some extra medical supplies from which he could replenish his lost equipment. So it was at Ning-po that there came word of the bombardment of Canton by the British fleet, and the start of the war between China and England which was not to end until four years later. On hearing about the news of war, Hudson's first concern, naturally, was for William Burns. He was, fortunately, no longer at Swatow, exposed to the rage of the hot-headed southern people. About all this, Hudson wrote his sister in November:

"As you are aware, I have been detained in Ning-po by various circumstances, and a sufficient cause has at length appeared in the disturbances which have broken out in the South. The latest news we now have is that Canton has been bombarded for two days, a breach being made on the second, and that the British entered the city, the Viceroy refusing to give any satisfaction. We are anxiously awaiting later and fuller accounts . . . I know not the merits of the present course of action . . . and therefore refrain from writing my thoughts about it. But I would just refer to the goodness of God in removing Mr. Burns from Swatow in time. For if one may judge of the feelings of the Cantonese in Swatow by what one sees here at present, it would go hard with anyone at their mercy."

So once again, something that seemed a great calamity one minute was soon seen to be included in the "all things" the apostle Paul said "work together for good for them that love God." And that was a lesson reinforced all the more by yet another development during Hudson's unplanned detention in Ning-po.

In the southern section of the city, near the ancient pagoda, was a quiet street, named Bridge Street, between two lakes. There Hudson's old friend and former colleague, Dr. Parker, had opened a dispensary a mile or two from his hospital. It was there, as autumn was advancing, that Hudson Taylor happily found a temporary home. Looking back on those days he later wrote:

"I have a distinct remembrance of tracing my initials on the snow which during the night had collected on my coverlet in the large, barnlike upper room. The tiling of a Chinese house may keep off the rain, if it happens to be sound, but does not afford so good protection against snow, which will beat up through the crannies and crevices and find its way within. But however unfurnished may have been its fittings, the little house was well adapted for work among the people, and there I thankfully settled, finding ample scope for service, morning, noon, and night."

The only other foreigners in that part of the city were Mr. and Mrs. J. Jones, also of the Chinese Evangelisation Society, and a Miss Aldersey who, with the help of two young English sisters, was running a surprisingly successful school for girls—the first ever opened in China. The sisters were the orphaned daughters of the Rev.

Samuel Dyer, one of the earliest missionaries to China.

When the Jones family had come to live not far from the school, the younger of the sisters, Maria Dyer, found many opportunities to help out and befriend the busy young mother. Whenever she could, Maria went out with the Joneses to do neighborhood evangelism, her fluency in the language proving a big help. Though she was not yet twenty, this bright, gifted girl had the heart of an evangelist.

That was no doubt one of the things about Maria that attracted Hudson Taylor's interest. For in the home of his fellow workers, he couldn't help but encounter Maria Dyer from time to time. And he soon found that he couldn't help but think of her even when he didn't encounter her. She had such a warm and open manner that the two young people soon became good friends. And before long she began to fill a place in his heart never filled before.

But before he was willing to admit his feelings, even to himself, outside circumstances interrupted their blossoming friendship. A plot to massacre all foreigners was discovered. Though the plan was thwarted, hostility among the region's Cantonese population toward the British was so widespread that the foreign community couldn't afford to ignore the danger. So it was decided that families with children would be sent to Shanghai, the port with the most secure foreign settlement. Hudson's familiarity with the Shanghai dialect made him the most logical escort for the party. As much as he hated to leave, he couldn't very well refuse the unwanted assignment.

Miss Aldersey could not be persuaded to leave Ningpo. Nearing retirement age, she was in the process of turning the management of her school over to the American Presbyterian Mission and didn't want any additional, unnecessary disruptions. So, taking what precautions were possible, she encouraged the Dyer sisters to remain in Ning-po with her. And since Maria's sister had just become engaged to his own special friend, J. S. Burdon, Hudson worried that Maria would feel all the more alone and unprotected.

Yet before he left for Shanghai, Hudson said nothing to Maria, or to anyone else, about his growing affection. Indeed he tried to deny it. For he had no reason to believe that she felt the same way about him and he wasn't anxious to have his heart broken again.

In addition, his time in China had shown him the kind of sacrifices required to carry out his call to evangelize the interior. And he had begun to realize lately how little security he had to offer a wife. His position with the Chinese Evangelisation Society was becoming more and more embarrassing. For some time he had known that the society was in debt and that his salary was being paid from borrowed funds. Recalling the circumstances, he later wrote:

"Personally I had always avoided debt, though at times only by very careful economy. Now there was no difficulty in doing this, for my income was larger, but the Society itself was in debt. The quarterly bills which I and others were instructed to draw were often met with borrowed money, and a correspondence commenced which terminated in the following year by my resigning from conscientious motives.

"To me it seemed that the teaching of God's Word was unmistakably clear: 'Owe no man anything.' To borrow money implied to my mind a contradiction of Scripture—a confession that God has withheld some good thing, and a determination to get for ourselves what he has not given. Could that which was wrong for one Christian be right for an association of Christians? Or could any amount of precedents make a wrong course justifiable? If the Word taught me anything, it taught me to have no connection with debt. I could not think that God was poor, that He was short of resources, or unwilling to supply any want of whatever work was really His. It seemed to me that if there were lack of funds to carry on work, then to that degree, in that special development, or at that time, it could not be the work of God. To satisfy my conscience I was therefore compelled to resign my connection with the Society . . . It was a great satisfaction to me that my friend and colleague, Mr. Jones . . . was led to take the same step, and we were both profoundly thankful that the separation took place without the least breach of friendly feeling on either side . . .

"The step we had taken was not a little trying to faith. I was not at all sure what God would have me do or whether He would so meet my need as to enable me to continue working as before . . . But God blessed and prospered me, and how glad and thankful I felt when the separation was really affected! I could look right up into my Father's face with a satisfied heart, ready by His grace to do the next thing as He might teach me, and feeling very sure of his loving care.

"And how blessedly He did lead me I can never, never tell. It was like a continuation of some of my earlier experiences at home. My faith was not untried; it often, often failed, and I was so sorry and ashamed of the failure to trust such a Father. But oh! I was learning to know Him. I would not even then have missed the trial. He became so near, so real, so intimate! The occasional difficulty about funds never came from an insufficient supply for personal needs, but in consequence of ministering to the wants of scores of the hungry and dying around us. And trials far more searching in other ways quite eclipsed these difficulties and being deeper brought forth in consequence richer fruits."

That winter thousands of homeless refugees poured into Shanghai from districts devastated by the ongoing Taiping Rebellion. Some of these sick, starving, often naked refugees lived in cemeteries where they found shelter by breaking into low arched tombs. Others crowded into any abandoned building, even those in ruins. And although Hudson took charge of one of the chapels of the London Mission and preached daily in the city temple, he went regularly out into the haunts of misery to care for sick refugees and to feed many of the hungry.

But no matter how busy he was, Hudson's thoughts turned constantly to Ning-po. Could God be in the feelings he was having? He had to be sure.

Back in Ning-po, unknown to Hudson, the one he loved was thinking just as much about him. And though Maria also prayed about her own growing feelings, she told no one but God. For she realized that no one else saw what she saw in Hudson Taylor. He was different from others—not more gifted or attractive, though he was bright, pleasant, and seemed to be fun-loving. There was something about him that made her feel rested and understood. He seemed to live in such a real world and to have such a real, great God. Though she hadn't seen that much of him during his time in Ning-po, she was startled to find how much she missed him when he left for Shanghai.

She heard others criticize his Chinese dress. But she loved it! At least she loved what it represented of his spirit.

She also respected his poverty and generous giving to the destitute. His vision to take the gospel to the interior was her vision as well—though it seemed so impractical for a woman.

So she thought and prayed about her friend during that long winter he was away in Shanghai, even though she had no assurance of his feelings for her.

Love finally conquered the silence. Hudson sent Maria a letter declaring his feelings and asking if she would consent to become engaged. The first thing Maria did when she got the surprise letter was to search out her sister and share her wonderful news. Then the two of them went to talk to Miss Aldersey, whose response was indignant.

"Mr. Taylor! That young, poor unconnected Nobody. How dare he presume to think of such a thing? Of course the proposal must be refused at once, and that finally."

Maria tried to explain how much she felt for him. That only made matters worse. Miss Aldersey decided Maria must be saved from such folly. The result was a letter, dictated by Miss Aldersey but written by Maria, not only closing the matter but requesting most decidedly that it might never be reopened.

Bewildered and heartbroken, Maria felt she had no choice. She was too young and inexperienced, and too shy in such matters, to stand up against Miss Aldersey's decision. And in the long, lonely days that followed, even when her sister was won over to Miss Aldersey's position, she prayed with the determined faith that nothing, nothing at all was too hard for the Lord. "If He has to slay my Isaac," she assured herself again and again, "I know He can restore." Yet she wondered if she would ever see Hudson again.

When Hudson did return to Ning-po that spring, the situation grew even more painful. Hudson, after the letter he received from Maria, could not attempt to see her; yet his feelings for her remained unchanged. And she had no way to let him know that the letter she had written wasn't any indication of her true emotions.

Meanwhile, Miss Aldersey, distressed at Hudson Taylor's reappearance, felt it her duty to disparage him in every possible way—not just to Maria but throughout the foreign community in Ning-po. His Chinese dress became the object of criticism and scorn. And his new status as independent missionary, not connected to any recognized mission, made him an even better target for criticism. He was accused of being "called by no one, connected with no one, and recognised by no one as a minister of the Gospel." Other insinuations soon followed: he was "fanatical, undependable, diseased in body and mind," and "totally worthless."

As a gifted and attractive young woman, Maria had no lack of other suitors who were openly encouraged by Miss Aldersey. At the same time, Chinese etiquette combined with his intention to honor the request of her letter, made it look impossible for Hudson to meet with Maria. Yet both young people continued praying for some indication of God's will.

Then one sultry day in July, at the end of an afternoon prayer meeting of missionary women at the Joneses' house, a storm swept up the tidal river and deluged Ning-po with sudden torrents of rain. Those women who hadn't left, including Maria Dyer and one of her closest friends, could do nothing but wait until the storm blew over. When Mr. Jones and Hudson returned to the house from the dispensary next door to learn that Maria and her companion were still waiting for sedan chairs, Hudson's friend, who knew about his feelings for Maria, said to him, "Go into my study and I will see what can be arranged."

A short while later Hudson's friend came downstairs to tell him that Maria and her friend were now the only ladies left. They were alone with Mrs. Jones and would be glad to see him.

Hardly believing his good fortune, his heart pounding in anticipation, Hudson went upstairs to see Maria for the first time in months. He saw nothing in the room but her face. And when he asked her permission to write to her guardian back in England, she quickly and eagerly consented. At the same time she let him know she felt the same love for him that he'd expressed for her. They recognized the obstacles still before them; but they determined together to keep praying for God's leading in their situation.

Finally knowing the truth of their mutual love brought indescribable joy to the young couple. But it did nothing for their patience as they waited for a response to Hudson's letter to Maria's uncle. And it made the continuance of Miss Aldersey's enforced separation seem all the more trying.

Four months stretched out like an eternity—especially when they knew Miss Aldersey had written home with the same accusations she'd been voicing around Ning-po. What if Maria's uncle was persuaded by her charges? What if he refused his consent to the marriage? Both young people felt that God's blessing depended on their obedience to those in parental authority. As Hudson wrote later:

"I have never known disobedience to the definite command of a parent, even if that parent were mistaken, that was not followed by retribution . . . The responsibility is with the parent in such a case, and it is a serious one. When the son or daughter can say in all sincerity, 'I am waiting for Thee, Lord, to open the way,' the matter is in His hands and He will take it up."

One day near the end of November patience and faith were both rewarded. The letter arrived. After careful inquiry, Maria's uncle in London had satisfied himself that Hudson Taylor was a missionary of unusual promise. The secretaries of the Chinese Evangelisation Society had nothing but good to say of him. And he got nothing but praise from other sources. So dismissing the unfair criticism for what it was, he cordially consented to his niece's engagement—requesting only that the marriage be delayed until she came of age. (Her twenty-first birthday would be in less than two months' time.)

Hudson could scarcely contain his excitement. He had to tell Maria the news. But how. Under the circumstances he couldn't rush to the school and ask to see her. There was in fact no place at the school appropriate for a private meeting to discuss their plans. And his own home was out of the question as well.

But when one of the missionary wives from the American Baptist Mission Board heard of his dilemma, she devised a plan to get the couple together. She lived in a quiet place outside the city wall and close to the river. She would send a note to the school asking Maria to visit her at her home. And if somebody else happened to be there when she arrived—well, such things happen.

So it was in Mrs. Knowlton's drawing room that Hudson waited while a messenger crossed the river to the school. Finally he heard Maria's voice in the hall, the door opened, and they were together, alone for the first time.

More than forty years later Hudson Taylor said of that moment, "We sat side by side on the sofa, her hand clasped in mine. It never cooled—my love for her. It has not cooled now."

Once they were publicly and officially engaged, they began making up for all the time they had been kept apart. Maria's birthday was on January 16; so the wedding was planned for the following week.

Several times that winter Hudson Taylor's finances dwindled to almost nothing. Once his funds were down to one twentieth of a cent before an unexpected shipment of mail arrived with additional funds from supporters back home. Encouraged as he was by such last-minute provision for his needs, he realized again how little he had to offer a wife.

He explained his precarious financial situation to Maria saying, "I cannot hold you to your promise if you would rather draw back. You see how difficult our life may be at times . . ."

"Have you forgotten," she interrupted. "I was left an orphan in a far off land. God has been my Father all these years; do you think I shall be afraid to trust Him now?"

"My heart did sing for joy," Hudson said, recalling the story. And his excitement is obvious in a letter he penned to his mother:

"I never felt in better health or spirits in my life . . . I can scarcely realise, dear Mother, what has happened; that after all the agony and suspense we have suffered we are not only at the liberty to meet and be much with each other, but that within a few days, we are to be married! God has been good to us. He has indeed answered our prayer and taken our part against the mighty. Oh may we walk more closely with Him and serve Him more faithfully. I wish you knew my Precious One. She is such a treasure! She is all that I desire."

And then, six weeks later:

"Oh, to be married to the one you do love, and love most tenderly and devotedly . . . that is bliss beyond the power of words to express or imagination to conceive. There is no disappointment there. And every day as it shows more of the mind of your Beloved, when you have such a treasure as mine, makes you only more proud, more happy, more humbly thankful to the Giver of all good for this best of earthly gifts."

8

"Oh, will not the Church at home awaken and send us out many more to publish the Glad Tidings?"

1858 - 1859

In the first months after their wedding, Hudson and Maria Taylor broke ground for a small home and headquarters in a rural district a few miles out of Ning-po. Surrounded by a large fishing population, they spent a happy month preaching of Christ to people who had never heard the gospel. But then they both contracted a fever, which turned out to be typhoid, and were forced to move back to the city to recuperate and find lodging for the hot summer months in some place where they wouldn't have to sleep on the ground floor.

So it was that the little house on Bridge Street, where Hudson had lived for a time as a bachelor, became a real home. Downstairs, the chapel and guest hall remained the same, and the Chinese Christians and inquirers came and went freely. But upstairs, the barnlike attic was transformed into cheery little rooms whose curtained windows looked out on the narrow street in front and the canal behind.

Maria Taylor, having lived in that neighborhood for five years, had friends everywhere among the people. Hudson soon realized what an advantage it was to their ministry that women and children could now be evangelized along with the men. And since "all the world loves a lover," the obvious affection and warmth evidenced by this young couple attracted old and new friends alike to the fellowship of their home.

One of their dearest friends and helpers was an ex-Buddhist leader, a cotton merchant named Mr. Ni. He had lived in Ning-po many years and was a deeply religious man. He spent much of his time and money in service to "the gods," yet he was satisfied by the religions he studied and taught to others.

Then, passing an open door on the street one evening, he heard a bell being rung and saw people assembling as if for a meeting. Learning that it was a hall for the discussion of religious matters, he too went in. Leading the meeting was a young foreigner in Chinese dress preaching from his Sacred Classics. The young man seemed at home in the Ning-po dialect, and Mr. Ni could understand every word of the passage he read. But what was its meaning?

"As Moses lifted up the serpent in the wilderness, even so must the Son of man be lifted up . . . For God so loved the world, that he gave His only begotten Son, that whosoever believeth in him should not perish, but have everlasting life. For God sent not his Son into the world to condemn the world; but that the world through him might be saved."

Mr. Ni was both puzzled and moved by what he heard. Saved, not condemned? A way to find everlasting life? A God who loved the world?

The meeting came to a close. The foreign teacher ceased speaking. And with the instinct of one accustomed to lead in such matters, Ni rose in his place, looked around at the audience, and said simply:

"I have long sought the Truth, but without finding it. I have travelled far and near, but have never searched it out. In Confucianism, Buddhism, Taoism, I have found no rest. But I do find rest in what we have heard tonight. Henceforth I am a believer in Jesus."

This new believer became an ardent student of the Bible. The rapid spiritual growth which resulted was a great encouragement to the Taylors. Not long after his conversion, he obtained permission to address a meeting of the religious society over which he had formerly presided. Hudson accompanied Mr. Ni on this occasion and was deeply impressed by the clarity and the conviction with which he preached. And when one of his former followers was led to Christ through his testimony, Hudson shared Mr. Ni's excitement at becoming a soul winner.

One day when talking with his missionary friend, Mr. Ni raised the question, "How long have you had the Glad Tidings in your country?"

"Some hundreds of years," Hudson replied.

"What? Hundreds of years?"

"My father sought the Truth," he continued sadly, "and died without finding it. Oh why did you not come sooner?"

It was a painful moment which Hudson Taylor would never forget. And it deepened his sense of calling. There was so much work to be done. He must still take the message of Christ into the interior of China where millions and millions still died every year without ever having heard the good news.

It was easy for Hudson to grow impatient with the work. What he really needed was more help. He was tempted by the prospect of hiring some of the new Chinese Christians to assist him full time. Already Mr. Ni was eagerly devoting all the time he could spare from his business. So were others from the growing band of converts: Neng-kuei the basketmaker, Wang the farmer of Hosi, and Tusi the teacher. Though they and others were all occupied in their necessary vocations through the day, they often came to the mission house in the evening and spent much time there on Sundays. It would have been easy to employ the Christian teacher in the school to which Maria Taylor was giving many hours daily. Or to take on others at a modest salary to train them for positions of usefulness.

But the Taylors decided that doing so, while it might prove a short-term help, could well be a hindrance to their goals in the long run. To pay young converts, however sincere, for making known the gospel—and to pay them with money from foreign sources—would surely weaken their influence in the community and perhaps also weaken their Christian character. How were the converts ever to know the joy of unpaid voluntary service, service out of love for the Lord, unless the missionaries could be patient and wait for their spiritual development?

So Hudson and Maria hoped and prayed that the time would soon come when the call of God into Christian service would become obvious to some of the Chinese Christians. And that when it happened the other Chinese Christians would themselves be ready and willing to support them. How was China ever to be evangelized but by the Chinese church?

In the meantime, the workload for the young missionaries became a never-ending challenge. Life was full and overflowing with both responsibilities and opportunities. Hudson himself did quite a bit of medical practice as well as regular preaching in the streets and in the chapel, receiving visitors, attending to correspondence and accounts, and continuing evangelistic excursions into the surrounding countryside. But none of those duties were allowed to interfere with what had become his chief task—the daily shepherding of his small but growing flock.

After the regular public meeting every evening, three

separate periods were devoted to carefully prepared study. To begin, Hudson would teach a lesson from the Old Testament. Then, after a time, a chapter was read from *Pilgrim's Progress* or some other helpful Christian book. And finally, a passage of the New Testament would be discussed and applied to daily life. This regular nightly schedule for the small band of Chinese believers led up to Sunday with its special services for worship and for reaching outsiders.

Sunday had its times of teaching too. For Hudson Taylor and his colleagues knew that it cost the Chinese Christians dearly to close up shop and store on the first day of the week. And they wanted to make the most of the time and sacrifice of the new converts. So between the regular services, Christians, inquirers, patients, school children, and servants were divided into classes and taught according to their particular needs. This made Sunday a heavy day for the missionaries, for there were only four of them—the Taylors and the Joneses—to share the great load.

But there was something unmistakable, almost tangible about their spirit of service and love for the people. It drew more and more people to the Bridge Street fellowship. Those who came brought others who also sensed the difference in that place—a difference one new visitor recognized when he asked the friend who had brought him, "Why does my heart feel so much wider when I come inside those doors?"

Perhaps it was because the Taylors' own hearts were as wide open as the doors of their mission to the people around them. For their ministry grew, and the promise of an even greater ministry grew with it.

• • •

The Treaty of Tientsin, signed in the summer after Hudson and Maria's marriage, opened the way at last to all the inland provinces. Foreigners now had the right to travel freely, under the protection of passports. Inland China, which Hudson had prayed about for so long, was now within reach. And yet more patience was required. He wrote home in November:

"You will have heard before this all about the new treaty. We may be losing some of our Ning-po missionaries . . . who will go inland. And oh, will not the Church at home awaken and send us out many more to publish the Glad Tidings?

"Many of us long to go—oh, how we long to go! But there are duties and ties that bind us that none but the Lord can unloose. May he give 'gifts' to many of the native Christians, qualifying them . . . for the care of the churches already formed . . . and thus set us free for pioneering work."

As anxious as Hudson and Maria both were to take the message of Christ to the interior, they each felt a prior commitment to the care and nurture of the small band of Ning-po Christians at Bridge Street. Leaving them now, even for the good of others, would have been like a parent abandoning young children in the wilderness.

Later years proved the wisdom of this decision. Many of these same poor and unlearned Chinese Christians were to become leaders and evangelists among their own people and provided invaluable service to Hudson Taylor in his life's work. But at this time, the Taylors' excitement over the spiritual and numerical growth of their little band of believers was mixed with an impatience to fulfill their greater calling—to the vast reaches of inland China.

Despite the open door to the interior and the changing

tides of the ongoing war (perhaps in part because of these factors), the widespread attitude toward foreigners remained hostile. The outrages of the coolie trade had spread northward and antagonized many people around Ning-po who heard tales of "devil foreigners" kidnapping men and boys and shipping them to far off lands—never to be seen again.

And while neighbors and friends might quickly come to the defense of the Taylors, the missionaries lived constantly with the threat that some rabble-rouser might one day incite a rioting crowd to take vengeance on any Europeans to be found. It had happened before in other cities and, given the underlying mood of the country, was almost certain to happen again.

While there wasn't much they could do for protection, the Taylors did keep a boat moored on the canal at the back door of their house, and a rope was kept firmly tied by their bedroom window that would allow them to escape to the canal under cover of darkness.

Such was the political situation during the second summer after Hudson and Maria were married when, after nine long months of expectant waiting, their first child was born. They named her Grace.

The thermometer read 104° F in the coolest part of the house on July 31, 1859, the day the little one was born. And only once in the week that followed did the temperature drop below 88° F—that was at midnight, during a thunderstorm.

The political climate remained just as hot. Surging crowds about the mission house had almost rioted a few days before. Cries of "Beat the foreigners" and "Kill the foreign devils" filled the air. But no one had beaten down the doors, as easy as that would have been.

Despite the continuing sense of danger, fear wasn't the feeling expressed in Hudson's next letter home. Instead he wrote:

"My dear parents: Though this is the Lord's Day I find myself able to pen a few lines, which will no doubt surprise you as much as it does myself. The reason is that I am at home taking care of my wife and baby-girl—your first grandchild! Oh my dear parents, God has been good to me, to us all! Better far than my fears, 'O magnify the Lord with me, and let us exalt His name together.' "

Though it was still some time before the period of dangerous unrest finally passed, the Taylors' joy over their new baby brought a wondrous new feeling of family into their lives. Yet even in this time of personal joy, there came a sad and unexpected occurrence which added greatly to Hudson Taylor's responsibilities and rooted him still deeper in his ministry in Ning-po.

Hudson's former colleague, Dr. Parker, had recently completed construction of his new hospital. Located strategically near one of the city gates overlooking the river, its impressive buildings attracted the notice of thousands daily. For the good doctor who had suffered with Hudson through their difficult beginnings in China, it was the wonderful culmination of years of patient work. The hospital, built to accommodate the needs of the foreign community as well as the doctor's Chinese practice, promised to be the foundation of the Parkers' ministry for years to come.

But suddenly the doctor's wife was stricken with a fever. Within hours she died, leaving her grief-stricken husband with the responsibility of caring for their four small children—one of them seriously ill. Dr. Parker saw no alternative but to take his children home to Scotland.

But what was to be done about his hospital? The wards were full of patients and the dispensary was crowded day after day with a steady stream of people needing medical help. No other doctor was free to take his place, and yet to close down with winter coming was unthinkable. To complicate things even further, there was no surplus of funds he could leave to continue the work. Yet he couldn't bear to see all his years of hard work and preparation go to waste.

Perhaps his young friend Hudson Taylor could carry on at least the dispensary portion of the work as a medical ministry to the local Chinese community. That was the proposition he laid before Hudson, who later recalled the experience:

"After waiting upon the Lord for guidance, I felt constrained to undertake not only the dispensary but the hospital as well, relying solely on the faithfulness of a prayer-hearing God to furnish means for its support.

"At times there were no fewer than fifty in-patients, besides a large number who attended the dispensary. Thirty beds were ordinarily allotted to free patients and their attendants, and about as many more to opium smokers who paid their board while being cured of the habit. As all the wants of the sick in the wards were supplied gratuitously, as well as the medical supplies needed for the out-patient department, the daily expenses were considerable. Hospital attendants also were required, involving their support. The funds for the maintenance of all this had previously been supplied by the doctor's foreign practise; with his departure this source of income ceased. But had not God said that whatever we ask in the name of the Lord Jesus shall be done? And are we not told to seek first the kingdom of God—not means to advance it—and that 'all these things' shall be added to us? Such promises were surely sufficient."

Since resigning from the mission which had sent him to China, Hudson had many opportunities to exercise that faith he had tried to build up during those years of preparation back in England—days which now seemed a lifetime ago and worlds away. And he was learning that God was just as faithful in China as he had been in England—where half-a-sovereign arrived in the mail the morning after Hudson had given his last coin to a starving family, and where Dr. Hardey's wealthy patient just happened to drop by to pay his bill at 10 o'clock on a Saturday night, in cash.

Just one illustration of God's earlier faithfulness needs to be told here:

Back when Hudson had been preparing to move from Shanghai to Swatow to develop the work he and William Burns had begun there, a Chinese servant he had hired to oversee the transportation of his household possessions disappeared with all of Hudson's earthly belongings. While by most standards the loss wasn't great (he estimated it at about forty pounds), it came at a time when Hudson was practically penniless and had no resources with which to replenish even the bare necessities for his survival and continued ministry in China.

Acquaintances had urged him to inform the proper authorities and have the man punished severely, but Hudson, who remained hopeful that the man would yet turn to God and repent, took a different course which he described in a letter home:

"So I have sent him a plain, faithful letter to the effect that we know his guilt, and what its consequences might be to himself; that at first I had considered handing over the matter to the ya-men [authorities], but remembering Christ's command to return good for evil I had not done so, and did not wish to injure a hair on his head.

"I told him that he was the real loser, not I; that I freely forgave him, and besought him more earnestly than ever to flee from the wrath to come. I also added that though it was not likely he would give up such of my possessions as were serviceable to a Chinese, there were among them foreign books and papers that could be of no use to him but were valuable to me, and that those at least he ought to send back.

"If only his conscience might be moved and his soul saved, how infinitely more important that would be than the recovery of all I have lost. Do pray for him."

Some time later, a copy of this letter Hudson had sent to friends in England came into the hands of George Muller, the great man of faith and founder of the Orphan Homes in Bristol, England. Muller was so impressed by the Christlike spirit of this young missionary he had never heard of, that he immediately sent to China a donation sufficient to cover Hudson's losses and continued to be a regular and generous supporter of Hudson's ministry as long as he lived.

But long before the gift from George Muller arrived, in fact, no sooner than he had written to forgive the man who had stolen from him, the mail arrived with a letter from Hudson's dear friends back in England—the Bergers. "Please accept the enclosed," Mr. Berger wrote, "as a token of love from myself and my dear wife." Inside was a check for forty pounds.

Having experienced God's faithfulness in such past situations, Hudson remained confident, even as he wrote:

"Eight days before entering upon the care of the Ning-po

hospital, I had not the remotest idea of ever doing so; still less could friends at home have foreseen the need." And those needs were many.

Right away Hudson informed the hired assistants who had been working for Dr. Parker that when current funds expired at the end of the month, the financial support for the hospital would have to be provided by God. When many of them accepted his permission to find other work, Hudson was suddenly in as much need of a staff as he was of money.

But when he shared this need with the Bridge Street Christians, many of them quickly volunteered their services. While the hospital's former employees weren't ready to believe in prayer as the ministry's only resource, the prospect didn't seem to bother Hudson's friends at all. Hadn't their teacher been telling them that God was a real Father who would never forget His children's needs? They gladly threw themselves into the volunteer work of the hospital. And the little fellowship of Christians immediately adopted the hospital and its concerns in prayer.

There were few secrets in China. And the financial circumstances of the hospital in Ning-po was no secret. In almost no time after Hudson had informed the old staff of the truth of the situation, the patients knew all about it. Soon the community at large had heard. And everyone waited to see what would happen.

As the days passed, what little money had been left by Dr. Parker was expended and Hudson's own supplies began to run low. There was much conjecture around town concerning the hospital's future. Naturally Hudson and Maria, along with their Christian friends, were continuously in prayer about it. Hudson realized this was a crucial test, with not just the continuation of the hospital but also the faith of many young believers at stake.

Day after day went by with no answer to their prayers.

Finally the morning came when Kuei-hua, the cook, appeared with serious news for Hudson. The very last bag of rice had been opened, and was disappearing rapidly.

"Then," Hudson replied, "the Lord's time for helping us must be close at hand."

And so it was. For before that bag of rice was finished a letter reached the young missionary that was among the most remarkable he ever received.

It was from Mr. Berger, and as before it contained a check—this time for fifty pounds. But this letter went on to say that a heavy burden had come upon the writer, the burden of wealth he wanted to use for God. Mr. Berger's father had recently passed away, leaving him a considerable increase of fortune. The son wrote that since he already had all the money required by his own needs, he was praying for guidance to know how the Lord might use this inherited money. Could his friends in China help him? The draft enclosed was for immediate needs. But he wanted them to pray about the matter and let him know if there was any way they could profitably use more.

Fifty pounds! There it lay on the table; and his far-off friend, knowing nothing about the last bag of rice or the many needs of the hospital, actually asked if he might send them more. Hudson Taylor was overwhelmed with thankfulness and awe. Suppose he had turned down Dr. Parker's offer to take over the hospital because of his lack of finances? Or lack of faith?

What a joyful celebration of praise the Taylors and their Christian friends had that day! And the patients marveled at the miracle.

Many of them said, "Where is the idol that can do anything like that? Have they ever delivered us in our troubles or answered prayers like this?"

9

*"To obtain successful workers,
not elaborate appeals for help, but first
earnest prayers to God to thrust forth
labourers, and second the deepening of the
spiritual life of the Church, so that
men should be unable to stay home,
were what was needed."*

1860 - 1865

Though the new hospital ministry was encouraging for Hudson and Maria, it also meant extra work and responsibility. When added to their already busy schedule, it took a serious toll on their time, energy, and health.

Soon after they assumed the management of the hospital, Maria wrote a letter to her husband's family back in England:

"Hudson has again been prevented from writing to you, which makes the fourth fortnightly mail since he was able to send off a letter. I hope you will not . . . I know you will not . . . begin to think that his dear little daughter is winning his heart away from his beloved parents. If he could steal some hours from the night he would do so, as he often has before, but his occupations leave him none to steal. He comes upstairs usually between ten and eleven o'clock, tired out with the long day's work, and after resting a little, down he goes again to see some of his patients or make up medicine for others . . ."

Some months later, his own energies draining even as the need and the opportunities for evangelism in China seemed to multiply, Hudson shared his own concern for needed assistance in a letter to his father:

"People are perishing, and God is so blessing the work. But we are wearing down and must have help . . .

"Do you know of any earnest, devoted young men desirous of serving God in China, who, not wishing for more than their actual support, would be willing to come out and labour here? Oh, for four or five such helpers! They would probably begin to preach in Chinese in six months' time, and in answer to prayer the means for support would be found."

Six years of ceaseless labor under the most difficult emotional and physical conditions had finally eroded Hudson Taylor's health. In the spring of 1860, he and Maria took a ten-day vacation in the country, hoping he'd be rejuvenated. But when they returned to the hospital, the work continued to sap his energy. Hudson began to suspect that he might be suffering from tuberculosis. In May he wrote home to his family:

"What I desire to know is how I might best serve China. If I am too ill to labour here and by returning home might re-establish health, if only for a time, or if I might rouse others to take up the work I can no longer continue, I think I ought to try."

The next month, as his health continued to decline, he wrote again saying:

"I trust, if it is the will of God, that I may be spared to labour for China. If not, all is well . . . Sometimes I think I may not live to see you; sometimes I hope to be spared to labour long and more earnestly than ever for China. All, all is known to Him who needs to know all . . . and He will do all things well."

Hudson grew weaker. So the Taylors sadly closed the Ning-po hospital and headed for Shanghai to book passage on a ship back to England. Leaving the Joneses to watch over their growing congregation of new Ning-po Christians, the Taylors planned to do what they could at home to stir up increased interest and concern for China. They prayed that their furlough from China would be short and that with proper medical care Hudson soon would be strong enough to return to the work they had begun.

But after a grueling, round-the-world voyage home, prospects for the future were not encouraging. Though it looked as though Hudson would eventually recover from his illness, his doctors told him he would never be strong enough to live and work in China again.

Hudson, refusing to accept their prognosis, continued to hope, pray, and work for the day he could return to China. In the meantime, he determined to do everything he could in England to contribute to Chinese missionary work.

He helped raise money for the Joneses and the ongoing work in Ning-po by writing many letters to would-be supporters, explaining to them what was happening in China. And with the blessing and support of the Bible Society, Hudson began the task of revising the "romanized" version of the New Testament in the Ning-po dialect. (While in China, the Taylors had found that it was much easier for less-educated Chinese to read and understand Chinese translations of books and Scripture which used a Western alphabet system with its twenty-six letters than to understand true Chinese writing with its thousands of characters.) And when his health finally permitted it, Hudson resumed his medical studies in London in hopes that if the time came when he could indeed return to China, he'd be even more useful as a fully qualified physician.

The appeal he made for four or five new missionaries before he left China had stirred much interest back in England. So for a time after arriving home, Hudson spent considerable time corresponding with a number of potential candidates. Only one young man finally went—James Meadows—and then not until 1862. But he went so much better prepared than Hudson Taylor had gone nearly ten years before. Hudson not only spent time orienting him before he left, but he undertook responsibility for the young man's financial support as well. And because he'd not forgotten the lessons of his first years in China, Hudson made sure James Meadows was dependably supplied with regular and sufficient support for his work.

The flurry of interest in China which was stirred up by Hudson and Maria's return soon faded. And because of the uncertainty of their future, the Taylors felt forgotten—half a world away from the work they longed to do, living on a dreary street in a poor section of London's east end.

Hudson, at age twenty-nine, and Maria, at twenty-four, must have felt at times as if life was passing them by as they lived in limbo, wondering what the future would hold. Not that their life in London was uneventful or unproductive. Their little daughter became a big sister to three younger brothers. And the Taylors learned more lessons in faith as they faced the constant challenge of trying to raise a growing active family on their very limited income.

Then there was the ongoing work of the Ning-po New Testament. Hudson had decided that the translation would be even more helpful if it would include marginal references and commentary in addition to the Scripture text. Fortunately he had the assistance of another veteran missionary to China from another mission society, and he had the invaluable services of Wang Lae-djun, a Chinese Christian who had voluntarily left his family and traveled back to England with the Taylors to help them on the journey and for as long as he could be useful.

Hudson and Lae-djun spent countless hours in Bible study and translation. A short excerpt from Hudson's journals shows the priority he placed on the task:

"April 27, Revision seven hours (evening at Exeter Hall).

" 28, " nine and a half hours.

" 29, " eleven hours.

" 30, " five and a half hours (Baptist Missionary Society meetings).

May 1, Revision eight and a half hours (visitors till 10 p.m.).

" 2, " thirteen hours.

" 3, " Sunday at Bayswater: In the morning heard Mr. Lewis, from John 3:33; took the Communion there in the afternoon. Evening, stayed at home and engaged in prayer about our Chinese work.

May 4, Revision four hours (correspondence and visitors).

" 5, " eleven and a half hours.

" 6, " seven hours (important interviews).

" 7, " nine and a half hours.

" 8, " ten and a half hours.

" 9, " thirteen hours.

May 10, Sunday: Morning, with Lae-djun on Heb. 11, first part, a happy season. Wrote to James Meadows. Afternoon, prayer with Maria about leaving this house, about Meadows, Truelove, revision, etc. Wrote to Mr. Lord. Evening, heard Mr. Kennedy on Matt. 27:42—'he saved others, himself he cannot save.' Oh, to be more like the meek, forbearing, loving Jesus! Lord make me more like Thee."

The meetings and interviews referred to in this journal were a big part of Hudson's work at that time. He was doing everything he could to convince denominational boards and existing mission societies to expand their efforts in China. He explained about the unprecedented opportunities now that foreigners could travel and live in the interior. He described his own experience and the welcome reception to the gospel he'd found during his years in China. He tried to impress everyone he talked to with the immensity of China, its millions of people, and their need of the gospel.

The Christian leaders he met nearly always gave the young missionary a sympathetic hearing. But it soon became evident that none of the boards were willing to assume the incredible challenge of evangelizing a country that contained half the non-Christian population of the entire world.

What could he do to stir up greater interest in China? Rev. W. G. Lewis, Hudson's friend and the editor of the *Baptist Magazine,* asked Hudson to write a series of articles about the work in Ning-po. The first article had already been published when Mr. Lewis returned the second manuscript. He told Hudson that he thought the articles were too important to be limited to publication in his small denominational magazine. "Add to them," he urged. "Let them cover the whole field and be published as an appeal for inland China."

Since Hudson had never forgotten his original calling to inland China, that's what he decided to do. He began studying in detail the spiritual needs of every part of China.

"While on the field," he wrote, "the pressure of claims immediately around me was so great I could not think much of the still greater need farther inland, and could do nothing to meet it. But detained for some years in England, daily viewing the whole country on the large map in my study, I was as near the vast regions of the interior as the smaller districts in which I had personally laboured—and prayer was the only resource by which the burdened heart could obtain any relief."

Every day Hudson looked at the map of China on his wall, read the promises in the open Bible that lay on his desk beneath the map, and prayed. Even as he labored to write a pamphlet, he prayed that it would inspire the Christian community of England to launch an unprecedented wave of missionary effort into China. He prayed for every part of his adopted land.

Compiling facts about the size and population of every province impressed Hudson all the more with China's need. At the same time, his research showed him an even more disturbing truth. In recent months the number of Protestant missionaries to China had actually been reduced from 115 to only 91. Something had to be done.

The more he prayed, the more keenly he began to feel that God wanted to use him to answer those prayers. But he was just one person. What could he do? Hudson didn't feel capable of what he now believed God was asking him to do. He wrote:

"I had a growing conviction that God would have 'me' seek from him the needed workers and go forth with them. But for a long time unbelief hindered my taking the first step . . .

"In the study of that divine Word, I learned that to obtain successful workers, not elaborate appeals for help, but first earnest prayers to God to thrust forth labourers, and second the deepening of the spiritual life of the Church, so that men should be unable to stay home, were what was needed. I saw that the apostolic plan was not to raise ways and means, but to go and do the work, trusting His sure promise who has said, 'Seek ye first the kingdom of God and his righteousness, and all these things shall be added unto you.'

"But how inconsistent unbelief always is! I had no doubt but that if I prayed for fellow-workers, in the name of the Lord Jesus Christ, they would be given. I had no doubt but that, in answer to such prayer, the means for our going forth would be provided, and that doors would be opened before us in unreached parts of the Empire.

"But I had not then learned to trust God for keeping power and grace for myself, so no wonder I could not trust Him to keep others who might be prepared to go with me. I feared that amid the dangers, difficulties, and trials necessarily connected with such work, some comparatively inexperienced Christians might break down, and bitterly reproach me for encouraging them to undertake an enterprise for which they were unequal.

"Yet what was I to do? The sense of bloodguiltiness became more and more intense. Simply because I refused to ask for them, the labourers did not come forward, did not go out to China: and every day tens of thousands in that land were passing into Christless graves! Perishing China so filled my heart and mind that there was no rest by day and little sleep by night, till health gave way.

". . . I knew God was speaking . . . Meanwhile a million a month were dying in that land, dying without God. This was burned into my very soul. For two or three months the conflict was intense. I scarcely slept night or day more than an hour at a time, and feared I should lose my reason. Yet I did not give in. To no one could I speak freely, not even to my dear wife. She saw, doubtless, that something was going on; but I felt I must refrain as long as possible from laying upon her a burden so crushing—these souls, and what eternity must mean for every one of them, and what the Gospel might do, would do, for all who believed, if we would take it to them."

For seven weeks that spring of 1865, Hudson Taylor made no entries in the journal he'd kept so faithfully. He was too consumed by the spiritual struggle going on in his heart and mind.

Summer came. The streets were hot and dusty in East London. Seeing that Hudson was not looking well, an old friend invited him down to the coast to spend a few days at Brighton. Maria, who was concerned about her husband's deteriorating health, encouraged him to go.

So it was a Sunday morning in Brighton that Hudson Taylor faced the greatest crisis yet in his life. He went to church with friends, but the sight of a large Christian congregation who heard the gospel every week only reminded him of the millions dying in China without ever having heard. Too upset to worship that morning, he walked out of the service and wandered out alone on the sands left by the receding tide.

As he walked, he rehashed the inner spiritual struggle that had gone on now for so long. He knew God was speaking to him. He felt confident that if he yielded to God's will and prayed for evangelists to go to inland China, God would answer and the missionaries would go. He believed, too, that God would provide the staggering financial needs for such a venture. Hudson had no doubts about that.

One question troubled him: What if they failed? He knew what new missionaries would have to face—the hardships and the challenges. What if they failed and blamed him? How could he assume that kind of responsibility? Later Hudson Taylor was able to analyze his struggle:

"It was just a bringing in of self through unbelief; the devil getting one to feel that while prayer and faith would bring one into the fix, one would have to get out of it as best one might. And I did not see that the power that would give the men and the means would be sufficient to keep them also, even in the far interior of China."

But at the time, on that beach in Brighton, he only knew a decision had to be made. He couldn't bear the conflict any longer. Would he accept the burden of leadership he felt God was asking him to take? He recalled later:

"In great spiritual agony, I wandered out on the sands alone. 'Well,' the thought came at last. 'If God gives us a band of men for inland China, and they go, and all die of starvation even, they will only be taken straight to heaven; and if one heathen soul is saved, would it not be well worth while?' "

It was then that another thought struck him: "If we are obeying the Lord, the responsibility rests with Him, not with us!" A great sense of relief flooded over him as he cried, "Thou, Lord. Thou shalt have all the burden! At thy bidding, as thy servant I go forward, leaving results to thee."

Of that moment, Hudson later wrote:

"There the Lord conquered my unbelief, and I surrendered myself to God for this service . . . Need I say that at once peace flowed into my burdened heart?

"Then and there I asked Him for twenty-four fellow-workers, two for each of the eleven provinces which were without a missionary and two for Mongolia; and writing the petition on the margin of the Bible I had with me, I turned homeward with a heart enjoying rest such as it had been a stranger to for months, and with an assurance that the Lord would bless His own work and that I should share in the blessing . . .

"The conflict ended, all was peace and joy. I felt as if I could fly up the hill to Mr. Pearce's house. And how I did sleep that night! My dear wife thought that Brighton had done wonders for me, and so it had."

But that was merely the beginning of an adventure of faith which was to see bigger trials and greater victories than Hudson Taylor had yet known.

10

*"Let us see that we keep God before
our eyes; that we walk in His ways and
seek to please and glorify Him in everything,
great and small. Depend upon it,
God's work, done in God's way,
will never lack God's supplies."*

1865 - 1866

Two days after his decision on the beach in Brighton, Hudson Taylor returned to London where his journal reads:

"June 27: Went with Mr. Pearse to the London & County Bank, and opened an account for the China Inland Mission. Paid in 10 pounds."

That was the first reference anywhere to the name of Hudson's new mission. And the money he put in its account was all the money he and Maria had. They were determined to trust God for their own support.

When he returned to London from Brighton, Hudson told Maria about the decision he had made and about the calling he had felt from God. Despite her frail health, her youth (she was still only twenty-eight), and the heavy responsibility she had for the daily care of their four small children, she accepted her husband's vision as her call as well. She committed her energies also to the seemingly impossible task of evangelizing the vast inland territories of China.

More than ever before in their seven and a half years of happy marriage, Maria became Hudson's comfort and inspiration—his constant encourager. She helped with his correspondence and records and prayed with him daily for their work and for the recruitment of the first party of missionaries they hoped to send out. She also collaborated with him on their most crucial task at hand, the completion of the publication their editor friend had suggested they write about the spiritual needs of China.

About the writing Hudson said, "Every sentence was steeped in prayer." And the prayers were answered. The pamphlet, which Hudson titled *China's Spiritual Need and Claims*, went so fast that it had to be reprinted just three weeks after publication. In the publication Hudson not only spelled out the needs of China, he reminded the Christian community of their responsibility, Christ's last directive on earth, to "go unto all the world." He called for twenty-four missionaries, and he spelled out the basis of the China Inland Mission which would guarantee no set salary for its missionaries who would trust God to supply their needs.

This "faith" mission idea seemed radical at a time when the only existing mission organizations were regular denominational boards. But Hudson's writing was so convincing that his pamphlet moved and inspired countless readers. Inquiries began streaming in from men and women interested in going to China. And though he deliberately avoided any appeal for financial support, readers began sending in money to be used in funding the work of the China Inland Mission's first missionaries.

The booklet also served as an introduction for the young, unknown Hudson Taylor to Christian leaders and potential supporters all over Britain. An example of readers' responses can be seen in this excerpt from a letter written by Lord Radstock:

"I have read your pamphlet and have been greatly stirred by it. I trust you may be enabled by the Holy Spirit to speak words which will thrust forth many labourers into the vineyard. Dear Brother, enlarge your desires! Ask for a hundred labourers, and the Lord will give them to you."

Hudson's prayer, which he recorded in his Bible, was

not for one hundred, but twenty-four missionaries for China. And the response to his appeal, while it must have been heartening on one level, added to his personal sense of responsibility. He was well aware that the task before him would prove a greater challenge to his faith than anything he'd yet done in his life.

However, it was Hudson's past experience of God's faithfulness that gave him the courage to proceed with his plans and helped inspire others to join in the work. Hudson's treatise told readers how he'd seen God answer prayer before—during storms at sea on his voyage to China, for his safety in China, and for the response of the Chinese people to the gospel. And it was his faith that shone through when he wrote:

"We have to do with One who is Lord of all power and might, whose arm is not shortened that it cannot save, nor His ear heavy that it cannot hear; with One whose unchanging Word directs us to ask and receive that our joy may be full, to open our mouths wide, that He may fill them. And we do well to remember that this gracious God, who has condescended to place His almighty power at the command of believing prayer looks not lightly on the bloodguiltiness of those who neglect to avail themselves of it for the benefit of the perishing . . .

"To those who have never been called to prove the faithfulness of the covenant-keeping God . . . it might seem a hazardous experiment to send twenty-four European evangelists to a distant heathen land 'with only God to look to'; but in one whose privilege it has been, through many years, to put that God to the test—at home and abroad, by land and sea, in sickness and in health, in dangers, necessities, and at the gates of death—such apprehensions would be wholly inexcusable."

The fact that there would be no set salaries made Hudson's mission distinctive enough. But he also opened its membership to volunteers from any denomination. He explained his thinking about the mission's makeup and organization this way:

"We had to consider whether it would not be possible for members of various denominations to work together on simple, evangelistic lines, without friction as to conscientious differences of opinion. Prayerfully concluding that it would, we decided to invite the cooperation of fellow-believers, irrespective of denominational views, who fully held the inspiration of God's Word and were willing to prove their faith by going to inland China with only the guarantee they carried in their Bibles.

"That word said, 'Seek ye first the kingdom of God and his righteousness, and all these things shall be added unto you.' If anyone did not believe that God spoke the truth, it would be better for him not to go to China to propagate the faith; if he did believe it, surely the promise sufficed. Again, we have the assurance, 'No good thing will he withhold from them that walk uprightly.' If anyone did not mean to walk uprightly, he had better stay at home; if he did mean to walk uprightly, he had all he needed in the shape of a guarantee fund. God owns all the gold and silver in the world, and the cattle on a thousand hills. We need not be vegetarians!

"We might indeed have had a guarantee fund if we had wished it; but we felt that it was unnecessary and would do harm. Money wrongly placed and money given from wrong motives are both greatly to be dreaded. We can afford to have as little as the Lord chooses to give, but we cannot afford to have unconsecrated money, or to have money placed in the wrong position. Far better have no money, even to buy bread with. There are plenty of ravens in China, and the Lord could send them again with bread and flesh . . . He sustained three million Israelites in the wilderness for forty years. We do not expect Him to send three million missionaries to China, but if He did He would have ample means to sustain them all.

"Let us see that we keep God before our eyes; that we walk in His ways and seek to please and glorify Him in everything, great and small. Depend upon it, God's work, done in God's way, will never lack God's supplies."

That declaration of faith, combined with the size of the task Hudson and his fledgling mission were taking on, drew the notice of Britain's Christian community. A lot of those who first heard the plans of this brash, unknown young missionary didn't quite know what to make of him.

But Hudson wasn't as concerned about his own countrymens' opinions of him as he was about the respect of the Chinese people. For that reason he persuaded the leaders of the Perth Conference to give him a chance to address the assembly. (The Perth Conference was an annual meeting of two thousand ministers and Christian leaders from all over Scotland.)

He began his address by transporting his audience half-way around the world, vividly recounting a true story of a journey he made in October, 1856, from Shanghai to Ning-po aboard a Chinese junk.

Among his fellow passengers had been a Chinese man who was educated in England and went by the name of Peter. As Hudson talked with him he learned that while the man knew the teachings of Christianity, he had never made a personal commitment to Christ. As Hudson and Peter began developing a friendship on this journey, Hudson had opportunities to talk to the man about his spiritual needs.

Spiritual Secret   127

As the junk approached the city of Sung-kiang-Fu, Hudson was in his cabin, preparing to go ashore to preach and distribute tracts when he heard a splash and then a cry of alarm that a man had fallen overboard. Rushing onto the deck, Hudson didn't see his new friend Peter. Was he the missing man?

"Yes," the boatman told Hudson, showing no concern. "He went down over there."

After convincing the reluctant captain to drop his sails, Hudson jumped over the side and began swimming back to the spot where Peter had disappeared. But the tide was running out, and the low shrubless shore provided no good landmark. His search seemed hopeless. Just then Hudson spotted some nearby fishermen with a dragnet—just what he needed.

"Come," he cried out in Chinese. "Come and drag over here. A man is drowning!"

"*Veh bin*," the fishermen replied. "It is not convenient."

"Come quickly or it will be too late," Hudson pleaded.

"We are busy fishing."

"Never mind your fishing. Come at once and I will pay you well."

"How much will you give us?" the fishermen wanted to know.

"Five dollars. But hurry."

"Too little!" they called back. "We won't come for less than thirty."

Hudson told them, "I don't have that much with me. But I'll give you all I have."

"How much is that?" they asked.

"I don't know. About fourteen dollars."

They finally brought their net over. The first time they passed it through the water they dragged up the missing man. But all Hudson's efforts to revive Peter failed. It was too late. The fishermen's indifference had cost him his life.

At the conclusion of that story a murmur of indignation swept over the crowd listening to Hudson. How could anyone be so callous and selfish?

That was the moment Hudson drove home his point:

"Is the body then, of so much more value than the soul? We condemn those heathen fishermen. We say they were guilty of the man's death—because they easily could have saved him, and did not do it. But what of the millions whom we leave to perish, and that eternally? What of the plain command, 'Go ye into all the world and preach the Gospel to every creature'? . . ."

Hudson went on to describe the incredible spiritual need of China. He compared Scotland, with its population of four million people and thousands of ministers, to China, with its four hundred million people and only ninety-one missionaries—less than one missionary for every four million people. He explained how, in the interior of China, there were regions as big as all Europe without a single minister of the gospel. He went on to tell his audience:

"It will not do to say that you have no special call to go to China. With these facts before you, you need rather to ascertain whether you have a special call to stay home. If in the sight of God you cannot say you are sure that you have a special call to stay at home, why are you disobeying the Saviour's plain command to go? Why are you refusing to come to the help of the Lord against the mighty? If, however, it is perfectly clear that duty—not inclination, not pleasure, not business—detains you at home, are you labouring in prayer for these needy ones as you might? Is your influence used to advance the cause of God among them? Are your means as largely employed as they should be in helping forward their salvation?"

At that point Hudson went on to recount that painful conversation with his Ning-po Christian friend Mr. Ni, when the ex-Buddhist leader had asked, "How long have you had the Glad Tidings in your country?"

Hudson had had to admit, "Some hundreds of years now."

And now he told that assembly of Christian leaders about Mr. Ni's pointed response. "Hundreds of years and you have never come to tell us? My father sought the Truth, and died without finding it. Oh, why did you not come sooner?"

Hudson continued his address to the Perth gathering:

"Shall we say that the way was not open? At any rate, it is open now. Before the next Perth Conference twelve million more, in China, will have passed forever beyond our reach. What are we doing to bring them tidings of Redeeming Love?

". . . the Lord Jesus commands us, commands us each one individually—'Go,' He says. 'Go into all the world and preach the Gospel to every creature.' Will you say to him, 'It is not convenient'? Will you tell him you are busy fishing—have bought a piece of land, purchased five yoke of oxen, married a wife, or for other reasons cannot obey? Will he accept such excuses? Have you forgotten that 'we must all stand before the judgement seat of Christ,' that every one may receive the things done in the body. Oh, remember, pray for, labour for the unevangelised millions of China, or you will sin against your own soul! Consider again whose Word it is that says:

" 'If thou forbear to deliver them that are drawn unto death, and them that are ready to be slain; if thou sayest, "Behold, we knew it not; doth not He that pondereth the heart consider it? And He that keepeth thy soul, doth not He know it? And shall not He render to every man according to his works?" ' "

With that challenge, Hudson ended his address. So powerful were his words and the conviction behind them that the great meeting was dismissed almost in silence. Who was this man who had such vision and faith?

Soon Hudson was being invited to speak in churches and at meetings all over Great Britain. And the people who heard his passion and vision for China responded to his message.

One thing, however, still troubled Hudson. He was concerned that his new mission might in some way deflect men or money from existing agencies. He felt that robbing Peter to pay Paul would do nothing to advance the kingdom of God. So he established standards that allowed the China Inland Mission to accept workers who might not be accepted by other missions, particularly those who hadn't completed university training. And furthermore, no one would be recruited or asked to join the mission. He believed that God would prompt those whom He wanted to volunteer.

In the same way, there were to be no appeals for money. Hudson trusted that if the mission could be sustained in answer to prayer, without donor lists or solicitation of any kind, it might grow up among the older societies without danger of diverting gifts from established channels. He believed the policy might even be helpful as an example to others that God would provide for those who obeyed him.

There wasn't much to the China Inland Mission in the way of formal organization. Hudson's long-time friends and supporters, Mr. and Mrs. Berger of Saint Hill, played an essential role which Hudson later explained by writing:

"When I decided to go forward, Mr. Berger undertook to represent us at home. The thing grew up gradually . . . Neither of us asked or appointed the other—it was just so."

A few essential spiritual principles were discussed with the candidates so that each principle was clearly understood as the basis of the mission. A few simple arrangements were agreed to in writing, in Mr. Berger's presence, and that was all. Again Hudson wrote:

"We came out as God's children at God's command to do God's work, depending on Him for supplies, to wear native dress, and to go inland. I was to be the leader in China . . . There was no question as to who was to determine points at issue."

Just as Hudson was to be in charge of the mission in China, Mr. Berger was responsible at home. He would correspond with candidates, receive and forward contributions, and publish a regular report and accounting of the work and its finances in what was to be called an "Occasional Paper." Mr. Berger would also send out suitable reinforcements as funds permitted and keep clear of debt. This last point was a cardinal principle Hudson felt strongly about. As he explained:

"It is really just as easy for God to give beforehand, and He much prefers to do so. He is too wise to allow His purposes to be frustrated for lack of a little money; but money obtained in unspiritual ways is sure to hinder blessing."

Nothing seemed to be hindering Hudson's plans for the new mission that fall. A number of candidates who had been accepted had moved to London and were being trained in the suddenly crowded Taylor home on Coburn Street. When the house next door promptly became vacant, the mission rented it and accommodations were doubled.

A letter Hudson wrote his mother in November spells out the level of activity going on at the time:

"The revision is now going on. We have reprinted the pamphlet (again), and have missionary boxes on the way. I am preparing a magazine for the mission, furnishing a house completely, setting up two fonts of type for China, teaching four pupils Chinese, receiving applications from candidates, and lecturing or attending meetings continually —one night only excepted for the last month. I am also preparing a New Year's address on China, for use in Sunday Schools, and a missionary map of the whole country . . . join us in praying for funds and for the right kind of labourers, also that others may be kept back or not accepted, for many are offering."

Prayers were being answered. Candidates for all twenty-four positions were accepted. And by the time the first "Occasional Paper" telling of plans and upcoming expenses for the voyage to China came off the press, the money was in hand. An insert had to be put in all the papers saying that the current needs of the mission had all been met.

In the early months of 1866, the last prayer meetings were held in the Taylor house on Coburn Street. Friends and supporters of the Taylors and of their first wave of missionaries to China crowded the rooms and staircase, sitting among the packing cases and bundles prepared for the journey. On the wall hung the map of China; on the table lay the open Bible.

Hudson Taylor had written of the new mission:

"Our great desire and aim are to plant the standard of the Cross in the eleven provinces of China hitherto unoccupied, and in Chinese Tartary."

Those who only saw the difficulties ahead shook their heads and called it "a foolhardy business."

Others who wished them well, sighed and said, "It's a superhuman task." And even their friends were anxious.

Some said, "You'll be forgotten. With no committee or organization before the public, you will be lost sight of in that distant land. Claims are many nowadays. Before long you may find yourself without even the necessities of life!"

But Hudson replied: "I am taking my children with me, and I notice it is not difficult to remember that they need breakfast in the morning, dinner at midday, and supper at night. Indeed, I could not forget them if I tried. And I find it impossible to think that our heavenly Father is less tender and mindful of His children than I, a poor earthly father, am of mine. No, he will not forget us!"

With that confidence, Hudson Taylor and his small band of young missionaries were ready to evangelize inland China.

11

"If we really wish to see the Chinese such as we have described, let us as far as possible set before them a true example. Let us in everything not sinful become Chinese, that we may by all means 'save some.' "

1866 - 1867

Hudson Taylor's band of young missionaries was marked by the same faith and sense of spiritual urgency that sustained him. That same confident commitment to God and to the challenge before them was evident from the very start of their journey. It shone forth from the correspondence sent home and from the results of their work and their lives.

For them, the simple theology of John 3:16—"God so loved the world, that he gave his only begotten Son, that whosoever believeth in him should not perish, but have everlasting life"—seemed motive enough to sacrifice their all. So the occasion of their leaving in May of 1866 deserved the tribute in verse penned by Hudson's missionary friend H. Grattan Guinness:

Over the dark blue sea, over the trackless flood,
A little band is gone in the service of their God;
The lonely waste of waters they traverse to proclaim
In the distant land of Sinim, Immanuel's saving Name.
They have heard from the far-off East the voice of their
    brothers' blood:
A million a month in China are dying without God.
No help have they but God: alone to their father's hand
They look for the supply of their wants in a distant land.
The fullness of the world is His; "all power" in earth and
    heaven;

They are strong tho' weak and rich tho' poor, in the
     promise He has given.
'Tis enough! they hear the cry, the voice of their brothers'
     blood:
A million a month in China are dying without God.

The party of sixteen missionaries plus the Taylors
with their four young children boarded the *Lammermuir*, a
small sailing ship of less than 800 tons, for a scheduled
four-month voyage around the globe. The first day on
board, the group unpacked and got their cabins in order.
But the second day the work began.

Hudson taught a Chinese language class every
morning. Then Maria taught another one in the afternoon.
There were times at the beginning when all the students
were down with seasickness; the teachers had to do double
duty as steward and stewardess. But the younger people
soon found their sea legs and proved to be good sailors.

Life can get very trying in the cramped quarters of a
small sailing ship. So it was easy for the crew to see how
consistently these young missionaries practiced what they
were going to preach in China. And while these rough
sailors were none too happy being stuck with a whole
boatload of missionaries, they soon became appreciative of
the group's friendliness, helpfulness, and even their
penchant for hymn-singing.

Although the missionaries themselves had prayed
beforehand for the opportunity to evangelize the crew, they
refrained from pushing their beliefs until the sailors
themselves asked if the missionaries would begin holding
services.

As Hudson wrote to his friends the Bergers:

"We commenced by having service on Sunday

morning in the Saloon with the captain's permission. A few of the sailors came. Then the young men started an afternoon meeting in the forecastle, held thrice weekly. Nor were our sisters less active. Mary Bell began a Bible class, which soon grew into a meeting for reading the Scripture and for prayer every night, Mrs. Nichols and others joining her. Some were converted, and these meetings became general . . . Miss Desgraz undertook reading with the four Swedes, Miss Faulding with a German, Miss Bausum with the cook and a South Sea Islander. Miss Barnes holds a reading-class for all who wish to improve themselves in English and has been blessed with the conversion of several."

Eventually a majority of the crew accepted Christ. One of the last was the first mate, Mr. Brunton, who had been a savage bully among the men. His sudden and complete change of heart and lifestyle was the cause of much excitement and rejoicing among the missionaries.

After a long, hard voyage across the Atlantic, through the treacherous waters at the tip of South America and then over the vast stretches of the South Pacific, the *Lammermuir* sailed safely. It wasn't until they reached the China Sea that the ship faced its greatest test.

For twelve straight days the ship was battered by one typhoon after another. Many among the crew were sick. The structure of the ship weakened. On Tuesday, September 18, they finally sighted the China coast, only to be hit by the worst weather yet. They encountered still another typhoon which drove the severely crippled ship away from their destination. The captain did all he could just to keep his ship afloat.

Hudson described the experience by writing:

"Friday, Sept. 21: The gale increasing and having all

the appearance of another typhoon, we had prayer together from time to time during the afternoon and night. The decks were swept by the sea in a manner I have never before witnessed.

"Saturday, Sept. 22: The jibs and stay-sails gave way early this morning. So fearful was the sea that the men refused to go out and secure them. The Captain and first Mate went on the forecastle . . . the men followed, but soon all had to be recalled as the vessel was driving into the sea. Soon after this the lee, upper bulwarks began to give way, and before long all this side was overboard. Next the jib-boom and flying jib-boom gave way, followed immediately by the foretop and top-gallant masts and the maintop-gallant mast. They hung by the wire shrouds, swinging about most fearfully, owing to the heavy rolling of the ship.

"The appearance of things was now truly terrific. The decks full of water, which poured over both sides as she rolled, were encumbered with floating spars, tubs, buckets, casks, etc. Besides the danger of being washed overboard, there was no small risk of having one's limbs broken by moving timbers torn from their moorings. Prayer to God was our only resource. The sailors, paralysed, gave up work. The probability seemed that our hours, if not minutes, were numbered. I kissed the dear children, and with the young men went out and set to work, hoping to encourage others."

Hudson downplayed his own role in the ship's survival. But another missionary, W. D. Rudland, wrote:

"All through the storm, Mr. Taylor was perfectly calm. When almost at its height the men refused to work any longer. The Captain had advised all to put on life-belts. 'She can scarcely hold together two hours,' was his verdict.

"At this juncture he was going to the forecastle where the men were taking refuge, revolver in hand. Mr. Taylor went up to him, 'Don't use force,' he said, 'Till everything else has been tried.'

"He then went in quietly and talked to the men, telling them he believed God would bring us through, but that everything depended upon the greatest care in navigating the ship, in other words, upon the men themselves. 'We will all help,' he added. 'Our lives are in jeopardy as much as yours.'

"The men were completely reassured by his quiet demeanour and friendly reasoning, and with officers, midshipmen, and the rest of us went to work in earnest at the wreckage and before long got in the great iron spars that were ramming the side of the ship."

Somehow the ship stayed afloat. The women, as well as the men, took turns on Sunday working the pumps to keep her that way.

It wasn't until Monday that the weather finally cleared. But the danger wasn't over. The pumps had quit and the ship was taking on water fast.

Yet throughout the ordeal, Maria Taylor, confined to her storm-tossed cabin with four young children, remained confident in God's steadfast grace. She later wrote:

"It was sweet to rejoice in God through all; to rest in past proofs of His love, independently of present circumstances; and I entered into Habakkuk's song as never before, 'Yet will I rejoice in the Lord; I will glory in the God of my salvation.' "

• • •

It wasn't until Sunday, September 29, that the *Lammermuir* limped into sheltered waters and anchored just offshore from the foreign settlement at Shanghai. Curious sightseers gathered to see the mangled, broken vessel that carried the largest single contingent of missionaries ever to arrive in China. But Hudson kept his worn-out band aboard for the night where the group held a praise service to thank God for his protection. (Another ship landing right after theirs reported the loss of sixteen out of a ship's company of twenty-two, yet no one aboard the *Lammermuir* was even seriously injured.)

Despite his gratitude for the safe journey, as he looked once again upon the city of Shanghai, Hudson must have felt that the real challenge was just beginning. None of the missionaries he knew there would be able to house a party of twenty people. And remembering how hard it had been to find accommodations just for himself the first time he arrived in China, he had to feel a great and sudden sense of responsibility for the young idealistic missionaries he brought with him. None of them knew what to expect when they stepped ashore in China for the first time. But Hudson knew all too well.

But just as prayers had been answered in the midst of the storm, they were also answered in Shanghai. A missionary acquaintance of Hudson's from Ning-po happened to have purchased a residence with an empty warehouse attached. He not only offered Hudson and his party the warehouse for temporary housing, he also told them they could store their extra printing, medical, and other supplies there when they journeyed inland. So it was only two days after the *Lammermuir* sailed into Shanghai that the entire mission party was housed and a temporary headquarters was established.

The group of missionaries caused a bit of a stir in the foreign settlement. Some Europeans seemed scandalized to learn that Hudson had brought ladies to China with the plan to send them into the unknown interior—and in Chinese dress no less. Some wondered if Hudson was some sort of madman.

It was indeed an unprecedented and bold venture. The Taylors had in their company a total of six unmarried women. At that time, in all of China, there were only seventeen single women missionaries, and not one was to be found outside the five treaty ports.

Hudson ignored the criticism, saying, "We have and may expect to have some trials . . . but the Lord is with us."

As to the criticism about his requirement that everyone associated with his mission should adopt Chinese fashion, Hudson remained convinced that it was the only way to carry out an effective ministry in the interior. Not only had his own experience proved that the strategy would reduce undue notice during travels into new territory, but he felt strongly that it would help reduce one more barrier to effective cross-cultural communication.

Evidence of just how visionary his thinking was on this subject can be seen in what he wrote to candidates in the first stages of applying to go out under the China Inland Mission. He wrote:

". . . I am not alone in the opinion that foreign dress and carriage of missionaries, the foreign appearance of chapels, and indeed the foreign air imparted to everything connected with their work has seriously hindered the rapid dissemination of the Truth among the Chinese. And why should such a foreign aspect be given to Christianity? The Word of God does not require it; nor, I conceive, could sound reason justify it. It is not the denationalisation but the Christianisation of this people that we seek. We wish to see Chinese Christians raised up—men and women truly

Christian, but withal truly Chinese in every right sense of the word. We wish to see churches of such believers presided over by pastors and officers of their own countrymen, worshipping God in the land of their fathers, in their own tongue, and in edifices of a thoroughly native style of architecture . . .

"If we really wish to see the Chinese such as we have described, let us as far as possible set before them a true example. Let us in everything not sinful become Chinese, that we may by all means 'save some.' Let us adopt their dress, acquire their language, seek to conform to their habits and approximate to their diet as far as health and constitution will allow. Let us live in their houses, making no unnecessary alteration in external form, and only so far modifying their internal arrangements as health and efficiency for work absolutely require.

"This cannot but involve, of course, a certain measure of inconvenience, such as the sacrifice of some accustomed articles of diet, etc. But will any one reflecting on what He gave up Who left Heaven's throne to be cradled in a manger; Who, having filled all things and wielded Omnipotence, became a feeble infant wrapped in swaddling cloths; Who from being the loved one of the Father—never misjudged, never unappreciated, and receiving the ceaseless adoration of all the hierarchies of Heaven—became a despised Nazarene, misunderstood by his most faithful followers, neglected and rejected by men who owed Him their very being and whose salvation He had come to seek, and finally, mocked, spit upon, crucified and slain with thieves and outlaws—will any follower of Christ, reflecting on these things, hesitate to make the trifling sacrifice indicated above?"

It was a sacrifice. And no one knew it better than

Maria Taylor. She wrote her friend Mrs. Berger:

"Things which are tolerated in us as foreigners, wearing foreign dress, could not be allowed for a moment in native ladies. I do not at all mean to imply a doubt as to the desirability of the change; but the nearer we come to the Chinese in outward appearance, the more severely will any breach of propriety according to their standards be criticised. Henceforth, I must never be guilty, for example, of taking my husband's arm out-of-doors! And in fifty or a hundred other ways we may, without great watchfulness, shock the Chinese by what would seem to them grossly immodest and unfeminine conduct . . . Pray much for us in respect to this matter."

Maria Taylor too had a cross-cultural sensitivity far ahead of her time.

• • •

Just three weeks after their arrival in Shanghai, the entire party boarded houseboats to travel together into the interior—heading up the Grand Canal toward Hangchow—in search of a permanent inland headquarters for the mission.

Traveling by houseboats made it possible for the women and children to be sheltered from curious crowds as they passed city after city. Everywhere they stopped Hudson inquired about permission to rent or buy accommodations where some of the young men in his party might settle. But at each stop he was refused permission from local authorities, no suitable place was available, the landlord wouldn't come to terms, or some other complication thwarted his original plan.

So the full contingent of missionaries, some twenty strong, remained together as the boats finally approached the great city of Hang-chow. The Taylors knew that two or three missionary families had already taken up residence in that city, and it would have meant serious risk to them as well as to the new arrivals if such a large party of foreigners stirred up opposition. But what else could they do? It was autumn; winter was fast approaching. The nights on the water were already bitterly cold. Several of the party were ill. And the boat people were clamoring to go home for the winter.

Never had the responsibility of leadership weighed so heavily on him as it did when Hudson left the boats in a quiet place outside the city and went ahead to inquire about the accommodation they so desperately needed. Maria also felt the seriousness of the situation. So after Hudson left she gathered the younger missionaries for prayer, telling them of the comfort that had come to her through the psalm in her regular reading that morning: "Who will bring me into the strong city? Who will lead me into Edom? Wilt not thou, O God? . . . Give us help from trouble; for vain is the help of man." Together they read that passage again as they waited anxiously for word.

Suddenly Hudson was back. Wonderful news. A home was ready, waiting for them. One of the Hang-chow missionaries was absent for a week and had left word that his house, comfortably furnished, was at the disposal of Mr. Taylor's party. Situated on a quiet street, it could be reached in the boats unobserved, and that very night the weary, thankful travelers were at rest in the great city.

Within the next few days, in spite of all the usual difficulties, Hudson secured premises of his own—a large rambling house which had once belonged to a government official, but had over time become a warren, occupied by a number of families. There was plenty of room to adapt to the needs of the mission party. A number of renters and their families stayed on for a while, making it possible for the group to begin missionary work within their own doors, without attracting too much attention. From the very start, Jenny Faulding, the youngest of the party, was already able to make herself understood by the Chinese women.

Hudson wrote in a report to his friends and supporters back in England at the first of December:

"It is pretty cold weather to be living in a house without any ceilings and with very few walls and windows. There is a deficiency in the wall of my own bedroom six feet by nine, closed in with a sheet, so that ventilation is decidedly free. But we heed these things very little. Around us are poor . . . heathen—large cities without any missionary; populous towns without any missionary; villages without number, all destitute of the means of grace. I do not envy the state of mind that would forget these, or leave them to perish, for fear of a little discomfort."

By mid-December, Jenny Faulding wrote home:

"We have been getting the house a little more comfortable though there is plenty still to be done. Mr. Taylor and the young men have contrived paper ceilings fixed on wooden frames, which keep out some of the cold air—for the upstairs rooms have roofs such as you find in Chapels at home. They also have prepared some of the partitions between the rooms. Of course we are as yet in confusion, but we are getting on, and I hope shall be settled some day.

"The lodgers are to leave next week. They occupy principally the ground floor . . . I am so glad for them to have been here, for many have come to Chinese prayer meetings and listened attentively. We could not have visited out-of-doors yet, . . . but I read and talk with those women every day and they seem to like it. One woman I have great hope of."

Before Christmas there were interested audiences of fifty or sixty at the Sunday services, and Hudson had made at least one evangelistic journey. In the neighboring city of Siao-shan, he and James Meadows had found excellent opportunities for preaching the gospel and had been able to rent a small house. They planned to settle some of the new arrivals there as soon as possible.

Right away Hudson wrote Mr. Berger at the home office:

"You will be glad to learn that facilities for sending letters by native post and for transmitting money . . . to the interiors are very good. I do not think there will be any difficulty in remitting money to any province in the empire which will not be easily overcome. In the same way, letters from the most distant parts can be sent to the ports. Such communication is slow and may prove rather expensive, but it is tolerably sure. Thus we see the way opening before us for work in the interior."

The team had barely established its first base in the interior and Hudson was already planning the next steps of sending missionaries farther inland. But in the meantime, his hands were more than full in Hang-chow. After the Chinese New Year, patients crowded into the dispensary, as many as two hundred a day, and an equal number attended the Sunday services. When the first reinforcements arrived from home early in 1867, Hudson was literally too busy to greet them until hours later. He was standing on a table at the time, preaching to a crowd of patients in the courtyard, and could only call out a hearty welcome as the newest party entered, escorted by James Meadows.

The business didn't seem to bother the new arrivals. They were more than happy to work side by side with the leader they so respected. John McCarthy, who became Hudson's chief medical assistant, later wrote of this time:

"I think of him as I ever knew him—kind, loving, thoughtful of everyone but himself, a blessing wherever he went and a strength and comfort to all with whom he came in contact . . . a constant example of all that a missionary ought to be."

Yet there was some dissension in the ranks. One couple critical of the Chinese dress policy stirred up complaints about Hudson's leadership from two or three others as well. But Hudson, and Maria, too, determined to respond with patience and love.

Though the handful of dissenters sent their complaints about the Taylors' leadership back to England, neither Hudson nor Maria felt it necessary to defend themselves. Not until months later did Maria mention the matter, even in writing Mrs. Berger. And then it was in answer to inquiries from Saint Hill that she wrote at length:

"Do pray for us very much, for we do so need God's persevering grace at the present time. We have come to fight Satan in his very strongholds, and he will not let us alone. What folly were ours, were we here in our own strength! But greater is He that is for us than all that are against us . . . I should be very sorry to see discord sown among the sisters of our party, and this is one of the evils I am fearing now . . . What turn the N—— matter will take I cannot think. One thing I know: 'the hope of Israel' will not forsake us. One is almost tempted to ask, 'Why was N—— permitted to come out?' Perhaps it was that our Mission might be thoroughly established on right bases early in its history."

Hudson and Maria were both deeply saddened by the conflict within the mission. Yet the response in Hang-chow continued to be very encouraging. So when the first baptisms came in May, Mrs. Taylor wrote again to Mrs. Berger:

"Perhaps the dear Lord sees that we need sorrows to keep us from being elated at the rich blessing He is giving in our work."

By that time the mission had established additional outposts and the administrative details had multiplied. As Jenny Faulding wrote:

"If only Mr. Taylor could be in three or four places at the same time it would be a decided advantage. He is wanting to visit the governing cities of this province, to look out the most eligible places for stations: he and Mr. Duncan have been on the point of starting several times. Then there is Ning-po where he is needed, and here he is overwhelmed with work. He wants to go to Shao-hing too (Mr. Stevenson's stations) that he may give further help with the colloquial dialect, there is hardly any knowing what his movements may be; yet he goes on so quietly and calmly always—just leaning upon God and living for others—that it is a blessing merely to witness his life."

The greatest sacrifice he had to make, Hudson felt, was leaving his family behind whenever he had to depart on a journey. He loved his children and enjoyed all the time he could spend with them—including the daughter who was born that first winter in Hang-chow. But his little eight-year-old daughter Grace seemed a particular blessing. During the voyage to China on the *Lammermuir*, she was so impressed by the changes she saw in the sailors who accepted Christ, that she made her own personal commitment to the Lord. After that, despite her tender age, she seemed as devoted to the task in China as her parents.

Early in 1867 she sent a note along with her father when he left on a short journey. Written on pink notepaper with a flower painted in one corner were the words:

"Dear Papa, I hope God has helped you to do what you wanted, and that you will soon come back. I have a nice bead-mat for you when you come home . . . dear, dear Papa."

As the summer malaria season set in and temperatures rose to 103° F indoors, Hudson took Maria, who was getting sick, and his five children out of Hang-chow to some nearby wooded hills where they rented a cooler summer shelter in the ruins of an old temple.

As they left their boats that first day and walked up the hill toward the temple, little Grace noticed a man making an idol.

"Oh, Papa," she said earnestly, "He doesn't know about Jesus or he would never do that. Won't you tell him?"

His daughter's hand clasped in his, Hudson did so. Afterwards they walked on and when they stopped to rest, Gracie wanted to pray for the man they had met. Hudson wrote:

"Never had I heard such a prayer. She had seen the man making an idol: her heart was full, and she was talking to God on his behalf. The dear child went on and on, pleading that God would have mercy upon the poor Chinese and would strengthen her father to preach to them. I never was so moved by any prayer. My heart was bowed before God. Words fail me to describe it."

Just a week later, a brokenhearted Hudson Taylor wrote to his friend Mr. Berger:

"Beloved brother, I know not how to write or how to

refrain . . . I am trying to pen a few lines by the couch on which my darling little Gracie lies dying. Her complaint is hydrocephalus . . .

"It was no vain nor unintelligent act when, knowing this land, its people and climate, I laid my wife and children with myself on the altar for this service. And He Whom so unworthily, yet in simplicity and godly sincerity, we are and have been seeking to serve—and with some measure of success—He has not left us now."

But to his mother, Hudson poured out his anguish:

"Our dear little Gracie! How we miss her sweet voice in the morning, one of the first sounds to greet us when we woke, and through the day and at eventide! As I take the walks I used to take with her tripping figure at my side, the thought comes anew like a throb of agony, 'Is it possible that I shall nevermore feel the pressure of that little hand . . . nevermore see the sparkle of those bright eyes?' And yet she is not lost. I would not have her back again. I am thankful she was taken, rather than any of the others, though she was the sunshine of our lives . . . But she is far holier, far happier than she could ever have been here.

"I think I never saw anything so perfect, so beautiful as the remains of that dear child. The long, silken eyelashes under the finely arched brows; the nose, so delicately chiselled; the mouth, small and sweetly expressive; the purity of the white features . . . all are deeply impressed on heart and memory. Then her sweet little Chinese jacket, and the little hands folded on her bosom, holding a single flower—oh, it was passing fair, and so hard to close forever from our sight!

"Pray for us. At times I seem almost overwhelmed . . . But He has said, 'I will never leave thee, nor forsake thee,' and 'My strength is made perfect in weakness.' So be it."

Spiritual Secret   *151*

12

*"Our God has brought us through.
May it be to live henceforth more fully to
His praise and glory. We have had another
typhoon, so to speak, not as prolonged as
the literal one, nearly two years ago, but at
least equally dangerous to our lives and
more terrible while it lasted."*

1867 - 1868

In a letter to his family in England, Hudson wrote that the only thing that kept his mind off his grief was the work he did with Maria. And they did work. Perhaps in determination not to let their daughter's death be for nothing, they devoted themselves anew to the task of reaching inland China with the gospel.

Before the close of 1867, little more than a year after their band of inexperienced missionaries had arrived in Shanghai, all the prefectural (governing) cities in Chehkiang had been visited. Nanking finally had been reached by a missionary, and the members of the mission were working in centers as much as twenty-four days' journey apart.

The church in Hang-chow was well established with Wang Lae-djun, Hudson's Chinese helper who had gone back to England with him, as its pastor. And by the spring of 1868, it looked possible for the Taylors to be spared from that center to help in expanding the work on some newer frontier.

In those days, opening any new mission station in China included the risk of death itself. Riots occurred so often that they became almost an accepted part of existence. So it seemed a natural and necessary question for Hudson to ask one missionary candidate, who had only one leg and could walk only with the help of a crutch, "But what would you do in China if a riot broke out and you had to run away?"

"I had not considered running away," the man answered quietly, and citing Scripture added confidently, "I thought that 'the lame' were to 'take the prey.' "

And in fact, after the man was accepted by the mission and helped open a new station in Wenchow, that confidence was tested. "Why don't you run away," yelled the rioters who were robbing him of everything he had and had even taken his crutches.

"Run away!" he replied with a smile. "How can a man run with only one leg, I should like to know!" Disarmed by his courage and friendliness, the rioters stopped their rampage, and calm was restored.

The same spirit of confident faith marked George Duncan, the tall, quiet Highlander who had made his way to Nanking as the first resident missionary there. The people of that city, which had felt the brunt of war as the old Taiping capital, remained so wary of any foreign interests that city officials sent word to all the innkeepers that the foreigner was not to be given any lodging.

Fortunately, the priest in charge of the city Drum Tower hadn't been warned—probably because no one considered him a possible host. Indeed, he had no proper room for visitors. But when a weary and discouraged George Duncan inquired, the man told him that he could stay in the tower at night if he wished, as long as he was out during the day so as not to frighten the people who came to the tower to worship.

It proved a particularly miserable place to live, but, wrote Duncan, "We gladly accepted it and managed very nicely, though we have rather more rats than I like. At night they want to devour everything." Between the constant scurrying of the rodents and the regular solemn sounding of the drums, the missionary didn't get much sleep. And at dawn he had to roll up his bedding and turn out on the streets to spend the day in tea shops and the marketplace sharing the gospel as best he could while trying to learn the local dialect. "I am not able to talk much," he wrote, "but God helping me I will say what I can . . ."

Eventually a local carpenter risked renting the foreigner a portion of an upstairs room where his own Chinese family lived. And not long after that, Duncan convinced the carpenter to rent a portion of a street-level room, which he partitioned off as a narrow little chapel—the first Christian church in Nanking.

Soon after his arrival in Nanking, George Duncan had sent Hudson the names of two banks that had representatives back in Hang-chow. But when one bank failed and the other left the city, there was no longer any channel for headquarters to provide him with the funds he needed to live and carry on his work.

Duncan didn't worry. Even when he had to change his last piece of silver and his Chinese cash quickly disappeared. But his Chinese cook and assistant became very concerned. "What shall we do when the money is all gone?" he asked.

"Do?" the missionary responded. "Why, we shall 'trust in the Lord, and do good.' So shall we 'dwell in the land' and verily we shall be fed."

Days went on, and still Hudson was unable to reach Nanking by native banks. Finally, in his anxiety for Duncan, he sent a brother missionary, W. D. Rudland, up the canal by boat with money for the work in Nanking. But the water level had dropped so far that by the time he sailed to a point that was still at least a week away from Nanking by canal, Rudland abandoned the boat and headed cross-country for a shorter, but more strenuous, four-day, sixty-mile walk to the city.

By this time, the cook's savings, willingly given to the work, had been completely used up. Duncan had not a dollar left. But he went out that morning to preach as usual, reminding his anxious companion:

"Let us just 'trust in the Lord, and do good.' His promise is still the same, 'So shalt thou dwell in the land, and verily thou shalt be fed.' "

That evening W. D. Rudland understood why the water in the Grand Canal had run so low. His overland hike brought him to Nanking several days earlier than would have been possible by boat. And when he reached his colleague's house, he found Duncan's cupboards as empty as his bank account. When Duncan returned tired and hungry from preaching all day, his Chinese helper went running to meet him.

"Oh sir," he cried breathlessly, "It's all right! It's all right! Mr. Rudland—the money—a good supper!"

"Did I not tell you this morning," Duncan replied, laying a kindly hand on the man's shoulder, "it is always 'all right' to trust in the living God?"

• • •

Hudson wasn't content to leave the challenges of pioneer missionary work to younger men like George Duncan. He and Maria readily faced as many dangers and hardships as anyone of those who worked for the China Inland Mission.

After only sixteen months of settled life in Hang-chow, the church there already numbered fifty baptized believers. But with Wang Lae-djun as pastor, and John McCarthy and Jenny Faulding assisting him there, the Taylors knew that the work was in good hands. So when spring came, Hudson and Maria packed up, loaded their household and four children aboard a junk, and set out by canal intending to join Duncan in Nanking or to establish another station in any city that might open up to them en route.

After living so long inside city walls, the freedom and freshness of the countryside provided a welcome and beautiful change of pace. Great mulberry plantations bordered the canal, with plum, peach, and apricot orchards blooming like some great bridal bouquet. Wheat and barley covered the lush valleys, which were interspersed with great fields of peas and beans in full flower. The canal itself, alive with boat traffic, fascinated the children just as the scenic beauty of its shores refreshed their parents.

For three weeks they traveled with Mr. Henry Gordon, one of their young missionaries who was just beginning his own new work in the famous city of Soo-chow-Fu, before their junk reached Chin-kiang at the junction of the Grand Canal and the mighty Yangtze River. So impressed was Hudson by the city and its strategic location that he determined to establish a mission station there. He began negotiations for property which the mission eventually acquired; but since the final details of the negotiations looked as if they would drag on for some weeks, the Taylors continued their journey up the northern segment of the canal.

So, after two months of boat life, the Taylor family reached the great city of Yang-chow, the city Marco Polo once governed. Its ancient, turreted walls enclosed a population of three hundred sixty thousand without even one missionary. Here again Hudson felt so burdened by the spiritual needs he saw that he decided to try to settle his family in Yang-chow.

About their arrival there, Maria wrote Mrs. Berger:

"Were it not that you yourselves are old travellers, I should think it impossible for you to realise our feelings last Monday week, when we exchanged the discomfort of a boat into every room of which the heavy rain had been leaking, for a suite of apartments in a first-rate Chinese hotel—such a place as my husband, who has seen a good deal of Chinese travellers' accommodations, never before met with—and that hotel, too, inside the city of Yang-chow."

Their reception by a friendly innkeeper and crowds of interested visitors greatly raised the Taylors' hopes for the promise of an effective new mission station in that great city. And when a favorable proclamation came from the governor on their behalf, they soon acquired a house into which the family moved in the middle of July.

The summer heat was already trying, and they hoped for quieter days in August. But the rush of patients and visitors continued. A foreign family seemed quite an attraction—especially as Hudson proved to be a skillful physician. Maria also established her own reputation among the women who were charmed by her pleasing Chinese speech and manners. Before long, just as had happened in Hang-chow, hearts began opening to the gospel. And the presence of a mother and children helped diffuse most suspicion.

But their success didn't come without trials or opposition. The children all contracted measles and the Taylors' youngest son developed a life-threatening case of bronchitis as a complication. Hudson himself grew so ill that for some time he wasn't at all sure he would survive.

During the summer some of the city's literati held a meeting and decided to stir up trouble. Anonymous handbills appeared all over the city, attributing the most revolting crimes to foreigners, especially those whose business it was to propagate "the religion of Jesus."

Before long the missionaries witnessed the changing attitude of the people. Friendly visitors gave way to crowds of disorderly rabble who congregated outside the Taylors' home, shouting insults at the missionaries. A fresh set of posters added fuel to the flame. Time after time rioting was prevented only by the kind, patient words of a sick, and very weakened, Hudson Taylor who stood in the doorway of his home, quietly answering all accusations and reassuring an angry mob that they intended no harm.

Finally, the intense heat of August was broken by torrential rains which effectively scattered the crowds. And the Taylors felt doubly relieved and heartened when the Rudlands and George Duncan arrived to help them.

However, the relief was short-lived. Two foreigners from Chin-kiang, Europeans in foreign clothing, came up to visit Yang-chow, causing quite a stir throughout the city. And those opposing the Taylors saw too good a chance to pass up. No sooner had the visitors left and everything returned to normal again, than the literati began circulating the rumor that children all over the area were reported missing. The story was that twenty-four children had been kidnapped by the inhuman foreigners. Everywhere the troublemakers were saying, "Let's avenge our wrongs! Attack! Destroy the foreigners! Much loot shall be ours!"

As a mob, intent on destruction, gathered outside the mission house, Hudson and George Duncan slipped away under cover of darkness and raced toward the governor's palace for help. As Hudson described it:

"But for the protection afforded us by the darkness, we should scarcely have reached the ya-men alive. Alarmed by the yells of the people, the gate-keepers were just closing the doors as we approached, but the momentary delay gave time for the crowd to close in upon us: the as yet unbarred gates gave way to the pressure and we were precipitated into the entrance of the hall. Had the gates been barred, I am convinced that they would not have been opened for us, and we should have been torn to pieces by the enraged mob."

Inside the governor's residence, Hudson and his friend were kept anxiously waiting. In the distance they could hear the sounds of a riot where they'd left the other missionaries, and Maria and the children, at the mercy of a mob that had already swelled to eight or ten thousand.

Finally the governor came out. Hudson pleaded for his help in calming the crowd and restoring order, and the official responded by calling out three thousand troops who soon dispersed the crowds.

Still fearful for the safety of the others, Hudson and George hurried back to the mission. Hudson wrote:

". . . we returned under escort. On the way back we were told that all the foreigners we had left were killed. We had to cry to God to support us, though we hoped this might prove exaggerated or untrue.

"When we reached the house, the scene was such as baffled description. Here, a pile of half-burned reeds showed where one of the attempts to fire the premises had been made; there, debris of a broken-down wall was lying; and strewn about everywhere were the remains of boxes and furniture, scattered papers and letters, broken work-boxes, writing desks, dressing-cases, and surgical instrument cases, smouldering remains of valuable books, etc.—but no trace of inhabitants within."

An agonizing search revealed that the missionaries and the children were hiding at a neighbor's house. After the rioters had broken in and begun burning the building, they had all escaped onto a roof and jumped to the ground in the darkness. Some had been injured—one young missionary man had received a serious head wound from a rock, Maria had injured her leg leaping from the roof, and others had various cuts and bruises—but they were all alive. And they were just as grateful to be found by Hudson as he was to find them.

As miraculous as their survival had been, Hudson decided not to take unnecessary chances. He loaded everyone on a junk and headed down the canal until passions cooled in Yang-chow.

Only forty-eight hours after the riot, as their boat neared Chin-kiang, Maria wrote in a letter:

"Our God has brought us through. May it be to live henceforth more fully to His praise and glory. We have had another typhoon, so to speak, not as prolonged as the literal one, nearly two years ago, but at least equally dangerous to our lives and more terrible while it lasted. I believe God will bring His own glory out of this experience, and I hope it will tend to the furtherance of the Gospel . . ."

The negotiations were long and difficult before the Yang-chow house was repaired and the missionaries permitted to return. But when they did, they received quite a reception. And it was with thankfulness that Hudson was able to write, "The results of this case will in all probability greatly facilitate work in the interior."

But it may have been the family life and friendly spirit

of the missionaries that gradually disarmed suspicion. "Actions speak louder than words," and neighbors had something to think over when the children were brought back after all that had happened, and when they learned that Maria was about to give birth again.

Despite the terror of their earlier exit from the city, she wrote to Mrs. Berger on their return to Yang-chow saying:

"In this again God has given me the desire of my heart. For I felt that if safety to my infant permitted it, I would rather it were born in this city, in this house, in this very room than in any other place—your own beautiful home not excepted, in which I have been so tenderly cared for, and the comforts and luxuries of which I know so well how to appreciate."

The arrival of a fourth son to Maria and Hudson indeed was a testimony to their Yang-chow neighbors. So was the speedy recovery of all who had been injured in the riot. As a result, the innkeeper who had first received them in the city, and two others who had dared much to befriend them during the riot, soon confessed belief in Christ and became candidates for baptism.

With great relief, Hudson and Maria assumed that the Yang-chow incident was over and done with. But that assumption turned out to be wrong.

13

"I have often asked you to remember me in prayer, and when I have done so there has been much need of it. That need has never been greater than at present."

1868 - 1869

During the turbulent summer in Yang-chow, Hudson Taylor sent a verbal message to the British Consul to inform him of the danger the missionaries faced. And shortly after that he sent a short note about his fears for the group's safety and the threats to their lives.

Though he called for no protection and expected none, word of the mistreatment of the China Inland Mission staff in Yang-chow triggered an international brouhaha that was to bring the two nations to the verge of war and severely threaten the ministry of the China Inland Mission.

Despite the recent treaty between the two countries that supposedly allowed anyone with a British passport to travel freely throughout China and take up residence anywhere in the country, British government officials and British merchants, as well as missionaries, regularly met with local opposition and sometimes outright hostility when they ventured beyond the original five treaty ports. Ever since the treaty had been signed, there had been a steady stream of complaints to the British Consul that in many parts of the country the Chinese were abiding by neither the letter nor the spirit of the treaty. At word of the unrest and threat to British missionaries in Yang-chow, the Consul (evidently waiting for just such an excuse) decided that the time had come to settle the issue once and for all.

Citing the reprehensible treatment of their nation's

subjects in Yang-chow, British officials in China, on instructions from the Foreign Office in London, seized the occasion to demand that China abide by the treaty. To back their demands made on the Chinese government in Peking, the British fleet made a show of force.

By the time reports of British demands and accounts of the accompanying saber-rattling reached London, a new government in England had replaced the one which had encouraged the aggressive policies in China. The new leaders in Parliament denounced the former government's China policy. And the loyal British press, half a world away and unable to check its facts, launched a bitter public attack on the missionaries who had brought the nation to the brink of war. The press accused the mission of demanding the protection of British gunboats in their campaigns to get the Chinese people to change their religion "at the mouth of the cannon and point of the bayonet."

For months the China controversy raged in Parliament and on the front pages of British newspapers. Quite naturally Mr. Berger at the home office of the China Inland Mission was pressed for an official response. But as he heard nothing from the Taylors about any appeals made to the British Consul for help, he could give no defense on behalf of the mission. He had to send inquiries to China asking for details and then wait months for an answer to return. Meanwhile public criticism of the mission and Hudson Taylor's leadership spread throughout England. This most recent news from China caused some financial supporters to stop giving to the China Inland Mission.

Maria Taylor, writing to relieve her husband, sent a long letter to the Bergers explaining all that had happened in Yang-chow. Concluding that letter she said:

"As to the harsh judging of the world or the more painful misunderstandings of Christian brethren, we generally feel that the best plan is to go on with our work and leave it to God to vindicate our cause. But it is right that you should know intimately how we have acted and why. I would suggest, however, that it would be undesirable to print the fact that Mr. Medhurst, the Consul General, and through him Sir Rutherford Alcock, took the matter up without application from us. The new Ministry at home censures those out here for the policy which the late Ministry enjoined upon them. It would be ungenerous and ungrateful were we to render their position still more difficult by throwing all the onus, so to speak, on them."

By this time Hudson, through his own negotiations, had managed to resettle the mission in Yang-chow. As to the storm that continued back in England, there was nothing to do but pray and wait for the criticism to die down.

In March the Yang-chow matter stirred passionate debate in the House of Lords where the Duke of Somerset went so far as to propose that all British missionaries be brought back from China before they cause any more trouble. And a concerned Mr. Berger wrote to tell Hudson:

"You can scarcely imagine what an effect it is producing in the country. Thank God I can say, 'None of these things move me.' I believe He has called us to this work, and it is not for us to run away from or allow difficulties to overcome us . . . Be of good courage, the battle is the Lord's."

At the same time this storm of criticism sprang up at home, another long-brewing crisis came to a head within the mission in China. The small group of missionaries who complained of Hudson's leadership and policies from the beginning had recently created more trouble by giving up their Chinese dress and subsequently getting expelled from the city where they were stationed. Hudson and Maria had graciously accepted them back at their own station, but when they still refused to take up Chinese dress and continued to oppose Hudson's leadership, he finally, with sadness, asked for their resignations. Though all but that handful of dissenters backed Hudson's decision, the malcontents' account of the problem, when it reached England, only added to the controversy and prompted even more supporters to reconsider their giving. This thrust the small mission into a state of crisis both at home and in China.

Hudson felt the strain and wrote home asking his friends:

"Pray for us. We need much grace. You cannot conceive the daily calls there are for patience, for forbearance, for tact in dealing with the many difficulties and misunderstandings that arise among so many persons of different nationality, language, and temperament. Pray the Lord ever to give me the single eye, the clear judgement, the wisdom and gentleness, the patient spirit, the unwavering purpose, the unshaken faith, the Christlike love needed for the efficient discharge of my duties. And ask Him to send us sufficient means and suitable helpers for the great work which we have yet barely commenced."

Despite the conflict and turmoil, the mission staff in China continued its pioneer evangelism in new territory. Even before the Yang-chow matters were settled and the mission returned there, Hudson had taken an important journey up the Grand Canal to a city from which he hoped to reach the northern provinces. And James Meadows had left his work in Ning-po to others that he might lead an advance into the first inland province westward from Chin-kiang—Anhwei—where there lived twenty million Chinese people without a single Protestant missionary.

But instead of the increasing numbers of missionaries and the additional finances they had been praying for to expand their work, the controversy at home drastically cut the financial resources the home office was able to send. Their prayers had to be answered in another, totally unexpected, way.

There lived a penniless man in England at the time—a man literally with no more resources than the birds of the air or lilies of the field—who was already supporting a family of two thousand orphan children without a cent of endowment, without an appeal of any kind for help, without even letting their wants be known to anyone but the Father in heaven. George Muller and his faith had for years been an inspiration to Hudson Taylor and to many others.

In addition to the demands of his own great work in Bristol, George Muller had always contributed to direct missionary work overseas. He regularly prayed for funds which he could use to help support the work of various missions—in China and elsewhere. He'd been contributing regularly and generously to Hudson Taylor's work for several years.

But no sooner had the Yang-chow riot taken place— long before the news could have reached England—than George Muller felt led to send extra money to the China Inland Mission. Within a day or two of the riot he wrote to Mr. Berger asking for the names of other additional members of the mission whom he might add to his list for ministry and prayer. Mr. Berger sent him six names from which to choose, and his choice was to take them all.

And that next year, when the shortness of funds in China was being most seriously felt, Mr. Muller wrote again, increasing his support. While that letter was still on its way, Hudson wrote to one of the mission workers:

"Over a thousand pounds less has been contributed during the first half of this (financial) year than last year. I do not keep a cook now. I find it cheaper to have cooked food brought in from an eating-house at a dollar a head per month . . . Let us pray in faith for funds, that we may not have to diminish our work."

Always more than willing to diminish his own comforts, Hudson intended never "to diminish our work." Within days he received George Muller's letter which said:

"My dear brother, the work of the Lord in China is more and more laid on my heart, and hence I have been longing and praying to be able to assist it more and more with means, as well as with prayer. Of late I have especially had a desire to help all the dear brethren and sisters with you with pecuniary means. This I desired especially that they might see that I was interested in them personally. This my desire the Lord has now fulfilled."

The eleven checks enclosed were for all the members of the mission Mr. Muller had not previously been supporting. Another letter from Mr. Berger arrived in the same mail:

"Mr. Muller, after due consideration, has requested the names of all the brethren and sisters connected with the C.I.M., as he thinks it well to send help as he is able to each one, unless we know of anything to hinder . . . Surely the Lord knew that our funds were sinking, and thus put it into the heart of His honoured servant to help."

It wasn't just the money George Muller sent that encouraged them. (Though Mr. Muller's donations to the

Spiritual Secret   169

China Inland Mission over the next several years amounted to ten thousand dollars annually—exactly the amount the mission's income had declined in the wake of the Yang-chow controversy.) It was knowing that this great man of faith was praying for their needs that made his gifts all the more encouraging. His words also bolstered the missionaries when he told them in the letter he sent with the first checks:

"My chief objective is to tell you that I love you in the Lord; that I feel deeply interested about the Lord's work in China, and that I pray daily for you.

"I thought it might be a little encouragement to you in your difficulties, trials, hardships, and disappointments to hear of one more who feels for you and who remembers you before the Lord. But were it otherwise, had you even no one to care for you—or did you at least seem to be in a position as if no one cared for you—you will always have the Lord to be with you. Remember Paul's case at Rome (2 Tim. 4:16-18).

"On Him then reckon, to Him look, on Him depend: and be assured that if you walk with Him, look to Him, and expect help from Him, He will never fail you. An older brother, who has known the Lord for forty-four years, who writes this, says for your encouragement that He has never failed him. In the greatest difficulties, in the heaviest trials, in the deepest poverty and necessities, He has never failed me; but because I was enabled by His grace to trust Him, He has always appeared for my help. I delight in speaking well of His name."

Such words were greatly needed by Hudson Taylor himself. While outwardly he appeared a solid rock, an inspiration to faith for all his young colleagues, the strain of responsibility grew heavier and heavier. Though reports of wonderful progress at new station after new station heartened him, the burden of the growing work weighed on his mind and heart. He couldn't seem to shake the deep inner depression that deprived him of any sense of peace.

Early in 1869 he exposed his heart and his hurt in a letter to his parents:

"I have often asked you to remember me in prayer, and when I have done so there has been much need of it. That need has never been greater than at present. Envied by some, despised by many, hated by others, often blamed for things I never heard of or had nothing to do with, an innovator on what have become established rules of missionary practise, an opponent of mighty systems of heathen error and superstition, working without precedent in many respects and with few experienced helpers, often sick in body and embarrassed by circumstances—had not the Lord been specially gracious to me, had not my mind been sustained by the conviction that the work is His and that He is with me in what is no empty figure to call 'the thick of the conflict,' I must have fainted or broken down. But the battle is the Lord's, and He will conquer. We may fail—do fail continually—but he never fails. Still, I need your prayers more than ever.

"My position becomes continually more and more responsible, and my need greater of special grace to fill it. But I have continually to mourn that I follow at such a distance and learn so slowly to imitate my precious Master.

"I cannot tell you how I am buffetted sometimes by temptation. I never knew how bad a heart I have. Yet I do know that I love God and love His work, and desire to serve Him only and in all things. And I value above all else that precious Saviour in whom alone I can be accepted. Often I am tempted to think that one so full of sin cannot be a child of God at all. But I try to throw it back, and rejoice all the more in the preciousness of Jesus and the riches of the grace that has made us 'accepted in the beloved.' Beloved He is of God; beloved He ought to be of us. But oh, how short I fall here again! May God help me to love Him more and serve Him better. Do pray for me. Pray that the Lord will keep me from sin, will sanctify me wholly, will use me more largely in His service."

Despite a faith that had brought him around the world to lead a mission into China, Hudson Taylor had never felt so inadequate and he had never desired God's help more.

14

*"I strove for faith, but it would not come;
I tried to exercise it, but in vain.
Seeing more and more the wondrous supply
of grace laid up in Jesus, the fullness of our
precious Jesus, the fullness of our
precious Saviour, my guilt and helplessness
seemed to increase."*

1869

Months passed. Hudson kept constantly on the move, his time divided mostly between the mission's two semi-official headquarters in Chin-kiang (where the mission's printing press was located) and Yang-chow (with its rapidly growing Chinese church). Summer brought yet another bout of serious illness that weakened Hudson for over a month. He hadn't even regained his strength before he embarked on yet another strenuous journey up the canal to provide medical care for Mr. Judd, who was dangerously ill himself. The Gordons, who were stationed in Soo-chow-Fu, came to consult with him about problems in their work. And the Duncans were on their way from Nanking for a special strategy session with the leader of the mission.

Hudson had never felt so worn-out, pressured, or discouraged. He clung desperately to the end of his physical, emotional, and spiritual rope.

Amid a pile of mail on Hudson's desk when he finally got back to Chin-kiang was a letter from his young friend and colleague, John McCarthy, written from the old home in Hang-chow. He knew something of Hudson's inner struggles because the two of them had talked about them the last time they were together. Since then he had made a spiritual discovery that he wanted to share with this friend and mentor. In his letter to Hudson he wrote:

"I do wish I could have a talk with you now, about the

way of holiness. At the time you were speaking to me about it, it was the subject of all others occupying my thoughts, not from anything I read . . . so much as from a consciousness of failure—a constant falling short of that which I felt should be aimed at; an unrest; a perpetual striving to find some way by which one might continually enjoy that communion, that fellowship, at times so real but more often so visionary, so far off! . . .

"Do you know, I now think that this striving, longing, hoping for better days to come is not the true way to holiness, happiness, or usefulness. It is better, no doubt, far better than being satisfied with poor attainments, but not the best way after all. I have been struck with a passage from a book . . . entitled 'Christ is All.' It says,

" 'The Lord Jesus received is holiness begun; the Lord Jesus cherished is holiness advancing; the Lord Jesus counted upon as never absent would be holiness complete . . . He is most holy who has most of Christ within, and joys most fully in the finished work. It is defective faith which clogs the feet and causes many a fall.'

"This last sentence, I think I now fully endorse. To let my loving Saviour work in me His will, my sanctification, is what I would live for by His grace. Abiding, not striving nor struggling; looking oft unto Him; trusting Him for present power; . . . resting in the love of an almighty Saviour, in the joy of a complete salvation 'from all sin'—this is not new, and yet 'tis new to me. I feel as though the dawning of a glorious day had risen upon me. I hail it with trembling, yet with trust. I seem to have got to the edge only, but of a boundless sea; to have sipped only, but of that which fully satisfies. Christ literally all seems to me, now, the power, the only power for service, the only ground for unchanging joy . . .

"How then to have our faith increased? Only by thinking of all that Jesus is and all He is for us: His life, His death, His work, He Himself as revealed to us in the Word, to be the subject of our constant thoughts. Not a striving to have faith . . . but a looking off to the Faithful One seems all we need; a resting in the Loved One entirely, for time and for eternity."

Hudson wrote afterwards about the impact of these words saying, "As I read, I saw it all. I looked to Jesus, and when I saw—oh, how joy flowed!"

And on his next trip to Yang-chow he hardly greeted his friends there before he began pacing back and forth across the room with his hands behind his back excitedly explaining what had happened to him. "Oh, Mr. Judd. God has made me a new man! God has made me a new man!"

And so it seemed to everyone who knew him. His friend Judd wrote:

"He was a joyous man now, a bright happy Christian. He had been a toiling, burdened one before, with latterly not much rest of soul. It was rested in Jesus now, and letting Him do the work—which makes all the difference. Whenever he spoke in meetings after that, a new power seemed to flow from him. Troubles did not worry him as before. He cast everything on God in a new way, and gave more time to prayer. Instead of working late at night, he began to go to bed earlier, rising at 5 a.m. to give time to Bible study and prayer (often two hours) before the work of the day began."

Only six months earlier Hudson had lamented his spiritual weakness saying, "I have continually to mourn that I follow at such a distance and learn so slowly to imitate my precious Master." But this was no longer an imitation. He now experienced the truth the apostle Paul described when he wrote that "Christ liveth in me." Instead of bondage, Hudson felt an exciting new freedom within; instead of failure, he sensed victory; instead of fear and weakness, he knew beyond doubt that his Lord would be sufficient. The difference seemed so amazing and so simple that Hudson wanted to share the secret with anyone and everyone he knew—starting with friends and loved ones.

To his sister Amelia Broomhall, whom he knew to be burdened by the cares and responsibility of a family that grew to ten children, he wrote:

"So many thanks for your dear, long letter . . . I do not think you have written me such a letter since our return to China. I know it is with you as with me—you cannot—not you will not. Mind and body will not bear more than a certain amount of strain, or do more than a certain amount of work.

"As to work—mine was never so plentiful, so responsible or so difficult, but the weight and strain are all gone. The last month or more has been, perhaps, the happiest of my life, and I long to tell you a little of what the Lord has done for my soul. I do not know how far I may be able to make myself intelligible about it, for there is nothing new or strange or wonderful—and yet, all is new! . . .

"Perhaps I may make myself more clear if I go back a little. Well, dearie, my mind has been greatly exercised for six or eight months past, feeling the need personally and for our Mission of more holiness, life, power in our souls. But personal need stood first and was the greatest. I felt the ingratitude, the danger, the sin of not living nearer to God. I prayed, agonised, fasted, strove, made resolutions, read the Word more diligently, sought more time for meditation—but all without avail. Every day, almost every hour, the consciousness of sin oppressed me.

"I knew that if only I could abide in Christ all would be well, but I could not. I would begin the day with prayer, determined not to take my eye off Him for a moment, but pressure of duties, sometimes very trying, and constant interruptions apt to be so wearing, caused me to forget Him. Then one's nerves get so fretted in this climate that temptations to irritability, hard thoughts, and sometimes unkind words are all the more difficult to control. Each day brought its register of sin and failure, of lack of power. To will was indeed 'present with me,' but how to perform I found not.

"Then came the question, is there no rescue? Must it be thus to the end—constant conflict, and too often defeat? How could I preach with sincerity that, to those who receive Jesus, 'to them gave he power to become the sons of God' (i.e., Godlike) when it was not so in my own experience? Instead of growing stronger, I seemed to be getting weaker and to have less power against sin; and no wonder, for faith and even hope were getting low. I hated myself, I hated my sin, yet gained no strength against it. I felt I was a child of God. His spirit in my heart would cry, in spite of all, '*Abba*, Father.' But to rise to my privileges as a child, I was utterly powerless.

"I thought that holiness, practical holiness, was to be gradually attained by a diligent use of the means of grace. There was nothing I so much desired as holiness, nothing I so much needed; but far from in any measure attaining it, the more I strove after it, the more it eluded my grasp, til hope itself almost died out, and I began to think that—perhaps to make heaven the sweeter—God would not give it down here. I do not think that I was striving to attain it in my own strength. I knew I was powerless. I told the Lord so, and asked Him to give me help and strength. Sometimes I almost believed that He would keep and uphold me; but on looking back in the evening—alas! there was but sin and failure to confess and mourn before God.

"I would not give you the impression that this was the only experience of these long, weary months. It was a too frequent state of soul, and that towards which I was tending, which almost ended in despair. And yet, never did Christ seem more precious; a Saviour who could and would save such a sinner! . . . And sometimes there were seasons not only of peace but of joy in the Lord; but they were transitory, and at best there was a sad lack of power. Oh, how good the Lord has been in bringing this conflict to an end!

"All the time I felt assured that there was in Christ all I needed, but the practical question was—how to get it out. He was rich truly, but I was poor; He was strong, but I weak. I knew full well that there was in the root, the stem, abundant fatness, but how to get it into my puny branch was the question. As gradually light dawned, I saw that faith was the only requisite—was the hand to lay hold on His fullness and make it mine. But I had not this faith.

"I strove for faith, but it would not come; I tried to exercise it, but in vain. Seeing more and more the wondrous supply of grace laid up in Jesus, the fullness of our precious Jesus, the fullness of our precious Saviour, my guilt and helplessness seemed to increase. Sins committed appeared but as trifles compared with the sin of unbelief which was their cause, which could not or would not take God at His word, but rather made Him a liar! Unbelief was I felt the damning sin of the world; yet I indulged in it. I prayed for faith, but it came not. What was I to do?

"When my agony of soul was at its height, a sentence in a letter from dear McCarthy was used to remove the scales from my eyes, and the Spirit of God revealed to me the truth of our oneness with Jesus as I had never known it before. McCarthy, who had been much exercised by the same sense of failure but saw the light before I did, wrote (I quote from memory):

" 'But how to get faith strengthened? Not by striving after faith, but by resting on the Faithful One.'

"As I read, I saw it all! 'If we believe not, he abideth faithful.' I looked to Jesus and saw (and when I saw, oh joy flowed!) that He had said, 'I will never leave thee.'

" 'Ah, there is rest!' I thought. 'I have striven in vain to rest in Him. I'll strive no more. For has not He promised to abide with me—never to leave me, never to fail me?' And, dearie, He never will.

"Nor was this all He showed me, nor one half. As I thought of the vine and the branches, what light the blessed Spirit poured direct into my soul! How great seemed my mistake in wishing to get the sap, the fullness out of Him! I saw not only that Jesus will never leave me, but that I am a member of His body, of His flesh, and of His bones. The vine is not the root merely, but all—root, stem, branches, twigs, leaves, flowers, fruit. And Jesus is not that alone—He is soil and sunshine, air and showers, and ten thousand times more than we have ever dreamed, wished for or needed. Oh, the joy of seeing this truth! I do pray that the eyes of your understanding too may be enlightened, that you may know and enjoy the riches freely given us in Christ.

"Oh, my dear Sister, it is a wonderful thing to be really one with a risen and exalted Saviour, to be a member of Christ! Think what it involves. Can Christ be rich and I poor? Can your right hand be rich and your left poor? Or your head be well fed while your body starves? Again, think of its bearing on prayer. Could a bank clerk say to a customer, 'It was only your hand, not you that wrote that cheque'; or 'I cannot pay this sum to your hand, but only to yourself'? No more can your prayers or mine be discredited if offered in the name of Jesus (i.e., not for the sake of Jesus merely, but on the ground that we are His, His members) so long as we keep within the limits of Christ's credit—a tolerably wide limit! If we ask for anything unscriptural, or not in accordance with the will of God, Christ Himself could not do that. But 'if we ask any thing according to his will . . . we know that we have the petitions that we desired of him.'

"The sweetest part, if one may speak of one part being sweeter than another, is the rest which full identification with Christ brings. I am no longer anxious about anything, as I realise this; for He, I know, is able to carry out His will, and His will is mine. It makes no matter where He places me, or how. That is rather for Him to consider than for me; for in the easiest position He must give me His grace, and in the most difficult His grace is sufficient. It little matters to my servant whether I send him to buy a few cash worth of things, or the most expensive articles. In either case he looks to me for the money and brings me his purchases. So, if God should place me in serious perplexity, must He not give me much guidance; in positions of great difficulty, much grace; in circumstances of great pressure and trial, much strength? No fear that resources will prove unequal to the emergency! And His resources are mine, for He is mine, and is with me and dwells in me.

"And since Christ has thus dwelt in my heart by faith,

how happy I have been! I wish I could tell you about it, instead of writing. I am no better than before. In a sense, I do not wish to be, nor am I striving to be. But I am dead and buried with Christ—ay, and risen too! And now Christ lives in me, and 'the life that I now live in the flesh, I live by the faith of the Son of God, who loved me and gave himself for me' . . .

"And now I must close. I have not said half I would, nor as I would, had I more time. May God give you to lay hold on these blessed truths. Do not let us continue to say, in effect, 'Who shall ascend into heaven?' (that is, to bring Christ down from above). In other words, do not let us consider Him as far off, when God has made us one with Him, members of His very body. Nor should we look upon this experience, these truths, as for the few. They are the birthright of every child of God, and no one can dispense with them without dishonouring our Lord. The only power for deliverance from sin or for true service is Christ."

It all seemed so simple and practical—as Hudson's sister discovered for herself.

"But are you always conscious of abiding in Christ?" someone asked Hudson many years later.

"While sleeping last night," he replied, "did I cease to abide in your home because I was unconscious of the fact? We should never be conscious of not abiding in Christ."

The discovery of this simple secret soon changed Hudson Taylor's life and ministry in ways he could never even have imagined before.

15

"I am more happy in the Lord than I have ever been, and enjoy more leisure of soul, casting more fully every burden on Him Who alone is able to bear all. To be content with God's will and way is rest."

1869 - 1870

Hudson had written, "I am no longer anxious about anything for He, I know, is able to carry out His will, and His will is mine." But that declaration of renewed faith was tested to its limits in the following few months as his duties piled up and storms of conflict again battered the little mission and its work.

A sampling of his correspondence hints at the load of responsibility he carried that fall. To one of the missionaries at Nanking he wrote on October 18, 1869:

". . . business is very pressing, but it does not hinder my joy in the Lord . . . I enclose the first six pages of your valuable little book, and am buying Chinese type to print it."

Later that day to another member of the mission he wrote, ". . . the mission funds are lower than they were before."

From Yang-chow on October 27 he reported: "Our work here is very encouraging at present. We cannot too much thank God for this. Five persons have been baptised . . . eight others are about ready to be received, and several more will, I trust, follow after a little time. It is the Provincial Examination at present, and the daily congregations are large and attentive . . ."

To another missionary at Tai-chow-fu on October 30: "I would ask you to remember funds in prayer; they are lower than they have ever been. Yet we are not and have not been forsaken, or lacking ever really; and we assuredly shall not be, if we have faith as a mustard seed . . ."

And in a letter to the new mission station at An-king the next day: "It occurs to me to add that some of the members of the Mission may be unaware of the amount of labour involved in serving them. It is a real pleasure, but it is none the less onerous. For instance, I have to write to Mr. Muller to thank him for your cheque; to Mr. Lord asking him kindly to sell it as he gets a better price than the Shanghai banks will give; then to enter it in his account and in my cash account; then to send the amount to Mr. Hart, with a note requesting him kindly forward it. Of course, I must also advise you of it, but this may not involve special writing. I thank God for permitting me to be a hewer of wood and drawer of water in His glorious work, and do cheerfully what little I can do to help, only regretting the impossibility of doing all that all wish. Just now I have seven different portions of Old and New Testament and long tracts sent me in several dialects, with requests to revise them. This, if possible at all, is the work of weeks if not months. Yet I am praying for guidance as to whether I may not have to leave tonight for one of our most distant stations, on account of a case of sickness."

Political unrest in China continually fanned the flames of fear, resentment, and hatred toward all Europeans, including missionaries. In November, word of a riot in An-king brought with it a rumor that all the foreigners in that city had been killed. And even after anxiety was eased by reliable reports that all the China Inland Mission missionaries and their small children had escaped An-king without injury, concern remained that this incident, like the Yang-chow riot would stir up even greater criticism at home. To his mother Hudson wrote:

"I am more happy in the Lord than I have ever been, and enjoy more leisure of soul, casting more fully every burden on Him Who alone is able to bear all. To be content with God's will and way is rest. Things may not be in many respects as I would wish them; but if God permits them to be so, or so orders them, I may well be content. Mine is to obey, His to direct. Hence I am not only able to bear up against the new trial at An-King but to be fully satisfied about it, not to wish it otherwise, but to thank God for it. 'Even so, Father, for so it seemed good in Thy sight.' Still, you will pray much for us all, will you not?"

Hudson and Maria spent a particularly happy Christmas that year, together with their children in Yang-chow. But their celebration didn't include the traditional English roast beef and plum pudding, according to a report by one of the newer missionaries, Mr. C. T. Fishe:

"They lived exclusively on Chinese food and I well remember the difficulty we had in hunting up a knife, fork, and spoon when a foreigner unskilled in the use of chopsticks came to Yang-chow. Condensed milk was not yet on the market, and they used few if any foreign items. There was one luxury, however—a big barrel of treacle [a form of molasses] that had recently come out on the *Lammermuir*. This was eaten with rice and much appreciated."

That season, as they had many times before, Hudson and Maria scrimped on their own personal expenses so they could share from their own accounts with the other missionaries under their leadership. And it wasn't just their money they were generous with, but also their time, attention, and concern, as Mr. Fishe indicated in writing:

"I . . . was much touched by Mr. Taylor's amiability. He was very kind to me. I helped him in his dispensary and medical work, and was with him a good deal whenever he was in Yang-chow. He guided my studies . . . He was of course, exceedingly busy, and appeared quite a young and lively man. He loved playing with his children, and did not seem burdened with care. He was fond of music and singing, and used to play the harmonium for the Chinese on Sunday evenings for an hour at a time, and have them sing hymns . . ."

Despite the pressures, Hudson and Maria seemed happier that fall and winter than ever before. Yang-chow had become more of a home for the entire Taylor family than any other city where they had lived in China. When duties called both parents away from home for a time, the children were left in the able and loving care of Hudson's secretary, Miss Emily Blatchley, who came out on the *Lammermuir* with the Taylors and had since become Hudson's personal secretary. But when the traveling parents would return, there were many warm and wonderful family reunions in that Yang-chow home.

Despite their great love for their children (and also because of their love), when spring came in 1870, Hudson and Maria made what was perhaps the most difficult decision in their married lives. There wasn't any school in China where the children could get an adequate education. And they dared not risk the heat and disease of another Chinese summer for their older children. They felt especially concerned about the deteriorating health of their five-year-old son, Samuel.

For a time the Taylors talked about Maria returning with the children to England. But Emily Blatchley volunteered to go to care for the children in England so Maria could stay and help Hudson continue the work. Though that seemed the wisest decision, the thought of separation from their four oldest children (the infant son born in the wake of the Yang-chow riot would be the only one staying with them) seemed a painful prospect for both parents.

But as the day for their parting approached, Hudson shared his emotions in a letter to his mother:

"God will provide. Oh, He is a Father! My precious Mother, you can enter somewhat into our feelings as this dark cloud draws near. Sometimes it seems, for a while, to take all one's strength and heart away, but God does and will help us. It is so good of Him to have given us to know more than we ever have known of His heart, His love, His gift, His joy, before calling us to take this step. He knows as we did not that we can do all things through Christ our Strengthener, and would not faint nor be ungrateful. And there are many mercies connected with this trial. Dear Miss Blatchley's love and self-sacrifice we can never repay. Next to ourselves, the children love her and she them. She knows just what our wishes are regarding them, in sickness and in health. I am sure you will do what you can to help her . . . and you will specially pray for my dear Maria. When all the bustle of preparation and the excitement of departure are over, then will come the trying time of reaction. But the Lord, Whose work calls for the separation, can and will support her."

As that day approached, Samuel's chronic illness grew worse. When he finally began to improve, the entire family set out by boat from Yang-chow en route to Shanghai to book passage for the children to England. But the boat wasn't even out of sight of Yang-chow when the little boy experienced a relapse. All night Hudson and Maria nursed their sick child. But at dawn the next morning, aboard that small boat floating down the middle of the great Yangtze River, Samuel slipped into unconsciousness and died.

Through a driving rain storm, Hudson and Maria crossed to the far side of the two-mile-wide river to bury their son in a little cemetery in Chin-kiang. As painful as the prospect of separation from their children was, Samuel's death and its reminder of the little girl they had already buried in Chinese soil confirmed in the Taylors' minds that their difficult decision was the right one for their children. The older boys and their little girl had to go back to England.

In Shanghai a few weeks later, after escorting the three children and Emily Blatchley aboard a French mail ship set to sail at daybreak, Hudson wrote to his friend, Mr. Berger:

"I have seen them, awake, for the last time in China. About two of our little ones we have no anxiety. They rest in Jesus' bosom. And now, dear brother, though the tears will not be stayed, I do thank God for permitting one so unworthy to take any part in this great work, not mine or yours; and yet it is ours—not because we are engaged in it, but because we are His, and one with Him Whose work it is."

Never had there been a more troubled time during all their years in China. But through it all the Taylors were confident that they made the right decision about their children. "I could not but admire and wonder at the grace that so sustained and comforted the fondest of mothers," Hudson wrote of Maria. "The secret was that Jesus was satisfying the deep thirst of heart and soul."

All manner of sickness raged throughout the China Inland Mission stations throughout that year. Before they even reached Chin-kiang again, after parting from the children, they were met with the news that Mrs. Judd was in that city at the point of death. Hudson couldn't leave the boat because of another critically ill patient on board. So it was decided that Maria would hurry ahead by land to Chinkiang to offer what help she could.

After days and nights of nursing his wife, Mr. Judd had come to the end of his own strength when he heard sounds of someone arriving in the courtyard below. Who could it be at that time of night and where had they come from? No steamer had passed upriver, and native boats would not be traveling after dark.

Maria Taylor, six months pregnant, having ridden all day over rough roads in a wheelbarrow, came rushing into the house. As Mr. Judd himself later recalled:

"Suffering though Mrs. Taylor was at the time and worn with hard travelling, she insisted on my going to bed and that she would undertake the nursing. Nothing would induce her to rest.

" 'No,' she said, 'you have quite enough to bear without sitting up at night any more. Go to bed, for I shall stay with your wife whether you do or not.'

"Never can I forget the firmness and love with which it was said—her face meanwhile shining with the tenderness of Him in Whom it was her joy and strength to abide."

The patient finally pulled through. But that disease-filled summer would yet take its toll on the mission. And an even greater danger threatened.

Hudson wrote: "Politically, we are facing a crisis. If our government continues their present, I almost said 'mad,' policy, war must result. In the meantime our position is becoming always more embarrassing . . . You can scarcely judge how intricate our path seems at times."

As the summer heat intensified, he wrote again to friends of the mission:

"We had previously known something of trial in one station or another; but now in all simultaneously, or near so, a widespread excitement shook the very foundations of native society. It is impossible to describe the alarm and consternation of the Chinese when they first believed that native magicians were bewitching them, or their indignation and anger when told that these insidious foes were the agents of foreigners. It is well known how in Tientsin they rose and barbarously murdered the Sisters of Charity, the priests, and even the French Consul. What then restrained them in the interior, where our brothers were alone, far from any protecting human power? Nothing but the mighty hand of God, in answer to united, constant prayer in the all-prevailing name of Jesus. And this same power kept us satisfied with Jesus—with His presence, His love, His providence."

In the wake of the Tientsin massacre, in which twenty-one foreigners were killed, the decision was made to send all the women and children out to the coastal cities. For a time it seemed as though the Chinese authorities might require them to leave the country altogether. The situation required much correspondence with officials, Chinese and foreign, and frequent letters to those workers most in peril. Meanwhile, the accommodations of the mission house at Chin-kiang were taxed to the utmost with extra boarders. So widespread was the unrest that no additional premises could be obtained.

"Old times seem to be coming round again," Hudson wrote to Emily Blatchley in June, referring to the now famous Yang-chow riot. "But with this difference—that our anxieties are not as before confined to one place."

By this time it looked as though all the river stations might have to be given up. The Taylors moved to Chin-kiang, since its location was more central than Yang-chow. Hudson himself slept on the floor in the sitting room or in a hallway every night so that Maria could share their room with other ladies. He wrote to Hang-chow near the end of June:

"One difficulty follows another very fast, but God reigns, not chance. At Nanking the excitement has been frightful . . . Here the rumours are, I hope, passing away, but at Yang-chow they are very bad . . . Pray for us much. My heart is calm, but my head is sorely tried by the constant succession of one difficulty after another."

In spite of the continuing illness, the political tension, and the expected arrival of a baby any time, Maria's work went on. In the hottest days of the summer she wrote Emily Blatchley to report:

"We have been holding classes on Sunday and two or three evenings in the week, to interest the Chinese Christians who can read in searching the Scriptures, and those who cannot read in learning to do so, and to set an example to the younger members of the mission who know pretty well that we have no lack of work. It may be a practical proof to them of the importance we attach to securing that the Christians and others about us learn to read and understand for themselves the Word of God."

Yet even in the midst of his growing troubles, Hudson's joy and excitement over his recent spiritual discovery remained evident to everyone around him. For example, after carefully answering questions from one of the mission workers about the continuing work in Yang-chow, he added these words of encouragement:

"And now I have the very passage for you, and God

has so blessed it to my own soul! John 7:37-39—'If any man thirst, let him come unto ME and drink.' Who does not thirst? Who has not mind-thirsts, soul-thirsts, or body-thirsts? Well, no matter which, or whether I have them all—'Come unto me and' remain thirsty? Ah no! 'Come unto me and drink.'

"What, can Jesus meet my need? Yes, and more than meet it. No matter how intricate my path, how difficult my service; no matter how sad my bereavement, how far away my loved ones; no matter how helpless I am, how deep are my soul-yearnings—Jesus can meet all, all, and more than meet. He not only promises me rest—ah, how welcome that would be, were it all, and what an all that one word embraces! He not only promises me drink to alleviate my thirst. No, better than that! 'He who trusts Me in this matter (who believeth on Me, takes Me at My word) out of him shall flow . . . '

"Can it be? Can the dry and thirsty one not only be refreshed—the parched soil moistened, the arid places cooled—but the land be so saturated that springs well up and streams flow down from it? Even so! And not mere mountain-torrents, full while the rain lasts, then dry again . . . but, 'from within him shall flow rivers'—rivers like the mighty Yangtze, ever deep, ever full. In times of drought brooks may fail, often do, canals may be pumped dry, often are, but the Yangtze never. Always a mighty stream, always flowing deep and irresistible!"

In yet another June letter he wrote:

" 'Come unto me and drink,' Not, come and take a hasty draught; not, come and slightly alleviate, or for a short time remove one's thirst. No! 'drink,' or 'be drinking' constantly, habitually. The cause of thirst may be irremediable. One coming, one drinking may refresh and comfort: but we are to be ever coming, ever drinking. No fear of emptying the fountain or exhausting the river."

Yet again, this new and deeper sense of faith would soon be tested.

• • •

On July 7, 1870, Maria gave birth for the seventh time. And Hudson wrote his parents telling them the news:

"How graciously the Lord has dealt with me and mine. How tenderly did He bring my loved one through the hour of trial, and give us our last-born, Noel. How I thanked Him as I stroked the soft, silky hair, and nestled the little one in my bosom! And how she loved him, when with a father's joy and pride I brought him to her for her first kiss, and together we gave him to the Lord."

But immediately upon giving birth, perhaps it had started even before, cholera struck Maria. She quickly grew too sick to nourish the baby, and before a Chinese wet-nurse could be found, the little baby died. Maria's own life hung precariously in the balance.

Hudson's same letter continued:

"Though excessively prostrated in body, the deep peace of soul, the realisation of the Lord's own presence and joy in His holy will with which she was filled, and which I was permitted to share, I can find no words to describe."

Maria herself chose the hymns to be sung at the baby's funeral. One hymn, "O Holy Saviour, Friend Unseen," seemed to linger in her mind.

Though faith and hope are often tried,
They ask not, need not aught beside;

So safe, so calm, so satisfied,
The souls that cling to Thee.
They fear not Satan or the grave,
They know Thee near and strong to save,
Nor fear to cross e'en Jordan's wave
While still they cling to Thee.

Weak as she was, Maria was not worried about her own health. At the age of thirty-three, she had always been strong. And she felt no pain.

She was far more anxious to hear word from England about their children than she was for her own health. When word came on July 21 in a letter from Mrs. Berger saying that all three children and Miss Blatchley had arrived safely at Saint Hill, it was the most comforting correspondence Maria had ever received. Even her friend's gentle and loving words gave her a sense of peace: "And now farewell, precious Friend," Mrs. Berger had written. "The Lord throw around you His everlasting arms."

Two days later, Maria Taylor took a turn for the worse.

16

*"I find increasing comfort in the thought
that all things are really in our Father's
hand and under his governance.
He cannot do but what is best."*

1870 - 1871

In the early morning hours of Saturday, July 23, 1870, Maria slept peacefully. So Hudson left her a few moments to prepare breakfast. While he was gone, she awakened and called out. He described his return to her side this way:

"By this time it was dawn and the sunlight revealed what the candle had hidden—the deathlike hue of her countenance. Even my love could no longer deny, not her danger, but that she was actually dying. As soon as I was sufficiently composed, I said:

" 'My darling, do you know that you are dying?'

" 'Dying?' she replied. 'Do you think so? What makes you think so?'

"I said, 'I can see it, darling. Your strength is giving way.'

" 'Can it be so? I feel no pain, only weariness.'

" 'Yes, you are going Home. You will soon be with Jesus.'

" 'I am so sorry,' she said, and paused as if half correcting herself for the feeling.

" 'You are not sorry to go to be with Jesus?'

"Never shall I forget the look with which she answered, 'Oh no! It is not that. You know, darling, that for ten years past there has not been a cloud between me and my Saviour. I cannot be sorry to go to Him; but it does grieve me to leave you alone at such a time. Yet . . . He will be with you and meet all your needs.' "

Little was said after that. A few loving messages to those back in England, a few last words about the children. Then Maria slipped into an unconscious sleep.

As the summer sun rose over the city, the hills, and the great Yangtze River, the busy hum of life spread throughout the streets and courtyards all around. But it was very quiet in that small upstairs room.

George Duncan's wife, who was staying with the Taylors, wrote:

"I never witnessed such a scene. As dear Mrs. Taylor was breathing her last, Mr. Taylor knelt and committed her to the Lord, thanking Him for having given her and for twelve and a half years of perfect happiness together, thanking Him too for taking her to His own presence, and solemnly dedicating himself anew to His service."

At 9 a.m. Maria Taylor took her last quiet and peaceful breath.

• • •

Earlier that same summer, Hudson Taylor had written, "My thirsty days are all past," claiming as true Jesus' promise, "He that cometh to Me shall never hunger; and he that believeth on Me shall never thirst." Could that promise hold true now?

Back on July 11, when his newborn son and Maria were both gravely ill, Hudson had written to his mother:

"I find increasing comfort in the thought that all things are really in our Father's hand and under his governance. He cannot do but what is best."

And now, on August 4, he wrote to her again saying:

"I have just been reading over my last letter to you, and my views are not changed, though chastened and deepened. From my inmost soul I delight in the knowledge that God does or permits all things, and causes all things to work together for good to those who love Him.

"He and only He knew what my dear wife was to me. He knew how the light of my eyes and the joy of my heart were in her. On the last day of her life—we had no idea that it would be the last—our hearts were mutually delighted by the never-old story of each other's love . . . and almost her last act was, with one arm around my neck, to place her hand on my head and, as I believe, for her lips had lost their cunning, to implore a blessing on me. But He saw that it was good to take her—good indeed for her, and in His love He took her painlessly—and not less good for me who now must toil and suffer alone, for God is nearer to me than ever. And now I have to tell Him all my sorrows and difficulties, as I used to tell dear Maria; and as she cannot join me in intercession, to rest in the knowledge of Jesus' intercession; to walk a little less by feeling, a little less by sight, a little more by faith."

And to Mr. Berger he wrote:

"When I think of my loss, my heart, nigh to breaking, rises in thankfulness to Him who has spared her such sorrow and made her so unspeakably happy. My tears are more tears of joy than grief. But most of all I joy in God through our Lord Jesus Christ—in His work, His ways, His providence, Himself. He is giving me to 'prove' (to know by trial) 'what is that good, and acceptable, and perfect, will of God.' I do rejoice in that will; it is acceptable to me; it is perfect; it is love in action. And soon, in that sweet will, we shall be reunited to part no more. 'Father, I will that they also, whom thou hast given me, be with me where I am.' "

Despite that confident faith, Hudson still felt his grief.

Especially when a new round of illness caused him long sleepless nights. He later wrote:

"How lonesome were the weary hours when confined to my room! How I missed my dear wife and the voices of the children far away in England! Then it was I understood why the Lord had made that passage so real to me, 'Whosoever drinketh of the water that I shall give him shall never thirst.' Twenty times a day, perhaps, as I felt the heart-thirst coming back, I cried to Him, 'Lord, you promised! You promised me that I should never thirst.'

"And whether I called by day or night, how quickly He came and satisfied my sorrowing heart! So much so that I often wondered whether it were possible that my loved one who had been taken could be enjoying more of His presence than I was in my lonely chamber. He did literally fulfill the prayer:

"Lord Jesus, make Thyself to me
A living, bright reality;
More present to faith's vision keen
Than any outward object seen;
More dear, more intimately nigh
Than e'en the sweetest earthly tie."

Later in August he wrote again to Mr. Berger saying:

"It is Sunday evening. I am writing from Mr. White's bungalow. The cool air, the mellow, autumnal beauty of the scene, the magnificent Yangtze—with Silver Island, beautifully wooded, reposing as it were, on its bosom—combine to make one feel as if it were a vision of dreamland rather than actual reality. And my feelings accord.

"But a few months ago my home was full, now so

silent and lonely—Samuel, Noel, my precious wife, with Jesus; the elder children far, far away, and even little T'ien-pao [the son born after the Yang-chow riots] in Yang-chow [where he was being cared for by a missionary wife]. Often, of late years, has duty called me from my loved ones, but I have returned, and so warm has been the welcome! Now I am alone. Can it be that there is no return from this journey, no home-gathering to look forward to! Is it real, and not a sorrowful dream, that those dearest to me lie beneath the cold sod? Ah, it is indeed true! But not more so, than that there is a home-coming awaiting me which no parting shall break into, no tears mar . . . Love gave the blow that for a little while makes the desert more dreary, but heaven more home-like. 'I go to prepare a place for you'; and is not our part of the preparation the peopling it with those we love?

"... I have been very ill since I last wrote to you, through a severe attack of dysentery my strength does not return rapidly. I feel like a little child . . . But with the weakness of a child I have the rest of a child. I know my Father reigns: this meets all questions of every kind. I have heard today that war has broken out in Europe, between France and Prussia; that it is rumoured that England joins the former and Russia the latter. If so, fearful doings may be expected; but 'the Lord reigneth.' "

Hudson's toddler son, T'ien-pao, suddenly became critically sick and the concerned father took him to an island off the coast in the hopes that the change of climate would save his life. He recovered only slowly. And even as Hudson tended to the needs of his last child left in China and prayed for his recovery, he thought often of his other children—a three-year-old daughter and the older boys who were eight and nine—halfway around the world.

"You do not know how often Father thinks of his darlings, and how often he looks at your photographs till the tears fill his eyes. Sometimes he almost fears lest he should feel discontented when he thinks how far away you are from him. But then the dear Lord Jesus who never leaves him says, 'Don't be afraid; I will keep your heart satisfied' . . . And I thank Him, and am so glad that He will live in my heart and keep it right for me.

"I wish you, my precious children, knew what it is to give your heart to Jesus to keep every day. I used to try to keep my own heart right, but it would always be going wrong. So at last I had to give up trying myself, and to accept the Lord's offer to keep it for me. Don't you think that is the best way? Perhaps sometimes you think, 'I will try not to be selfish or unkind or disobedient.' And yet, though you really try, you do not succeed. But Jesus says: 'You should trust that to Me. I would keep that little heart, if you would trust Me with it.' And he would, too.

"Once I used to try to think very much and very often about Jesus, but I often forgot Him. Now I trust Jesus to keep my heart remembering Him, and He does so. This is the best way. Ask dear Miss Blatchley to tell you more about His way, and pray God to make it plain to you, and to help you so trust Jesus."

To Miss Blatchley Hudson had written after Maria's death saying:

"You will love them all the more now that they can never again know a mother's care. God will help you to bear with them, and to try to correct them by lovingly pointing out the right way rather than by too frequent reproof—'Don't do this or that.' This I feel is where I most failed with them; and now, there is only you to make up for my deficiencies."

To his children he wrote yet again:

"My darling treasures—It is not very long since my last letter, but I want to write again. I wonder if you will try to write me a little answer? . . . I have been thinking tonight—if Jesus makes me so happy by always keeping near me, and talking to me every minute or two though I cannot see Him, how happy darling Mamma must be! I am so glad for her to be with Him . . . I shall be so glad to go to her when Jesus thinks it best. But I hope He will help me to be equally willing to live with Him here, so long as He has any work for me to do for Him and for poor China.

"Now, my darling children, I want you to love Jesus very much, and to know that He really does love you very much. Don't you think your far-off, dear Papa would be very pleased to see you and talk to you, and to take you on his knee and kiss you? You know he would! Well, Jesus will always be far more pleased when you think of Him with loving thoughts, and speak to Him with loving words. Don't think of Him as some dreadful Being. Think of Him as very good and very great, able to do everything, but as very gentle and very kind. When you wake, say to Him, either aloud or in your hearts:

" 'Good morning, dear Jesus. I am so glad you have been by me all night, and have taken care of me. Teach me how much you love me. Take care of my heart: make it think good thoughts. Take care of my lips: only let them speak kind, good words. Help me always to know what is right and to do it.'

"He likes us to talk to Him. When I am walking alone, I often talk aloud to Him. At other times I talk to Him in my heart. Do not forget, my darling children, that He is always with you. Awake or asleep, at home or elsewhere. He is really with you though you cannot see Him. So I hope you will try not to grieve so constant and kind a friend."

To Emily Blatchley he added:

"I have written again to the dear children. I do long for them to learn early . . . the precious truths which have come so late to me concerning oneness with and the indwelling of Christ. These do not seem to me more difficult of apprehension than the truths of redemption. Both need the teaching of the Spirit, nothing more. May God help you to live Christ before these little ones, and to minister Him to them. How wonderfully He has led and taught us! How little I believed the rest and peace of heart I now enjoy were possible down here! It is heaven begun below, is it not? . . . Compared with this union with Christ, heaven or earth are unimportant accidents."

There was, meanwhile, no easing of tensions in China. The claims made by European countries concerning the Tientsin massacre were being ignored by the Chinese government. Knowing that Europe was consumed by war, the Chinese authorities did nothing to ease the anti-foreign agitation. Hudson spelled out the seriousness of the situation in a letter he sent out at the end of the year calling friends and supporters to unite on December 31 in a day of fasting and prayer for China. He wrote:

"The present year has been in many ways remarkable. Perhaps every one of our number has been more or less face to face with danger, perplexity, and distress. But out of it all the Lord has delivered us. And some who have drunk more deeply than ever before the cup of the Man of Sorrows can testify that it has been a most blessed year to our souls and can give God thanks for it. Personally, it has been the most sorrowful and the most blessed year of my life, and I doubt not that others have had in some measure the same experience. We have put to the proof the faithfulness of God—His power to support in trouble and to give patience under affliction, as well as to deliver from danger. And should greater dangers await us, should deeper sorrows come . . . it is to be hoped that they will be met in a strengthened confidence in our God.

"We have great cause for thankfulness in one respect: we have been so situated as to show the Chinese Christians that our position, as well as theirs, has been and may again be one of danger. They have been helped, doubtless, to look from 'foreign power' to God Himself for protection by the fact that (1) the former has been felt to be uncertain and unreliable . . . and (2) that we have been in calmness and joy in our various positions of duty. If in any measure we have failed to rest, for ourselves, in God's power to sustain us in or protect us from danger, as He sees best, let us humbly confess this, and all conscious failure, to our faithful covenant-keeping God . . .

"I trust we are all fully satisfied that we are God's servants, sent by Him to the various posts we occupy, and that we are doing His work in them. He set before us the open doors we have entered, and in past times of excitement He has preserved us. We did not come to China because missionary work here was either safe or easy, but because He had called us. We did not enter upon our present positions under a guarantee of human protection, but relying on the promise of His presence. The accidents of ease or difficulty, of apparent safety or danger, of man's approval or disapproval, in no wise affect our duty. Should circumstances arise involving us in what may seem special danger, we shall have grace, I trust, to manifest the depth and reality of our confidence in Him, and by faithfulness to our charge to prove that we are followers of the Good Shepherd who did not flee from death itself . . . But if we would manifest such a spirit then, we must seek the needed grace now. It is too late to look for arms and begin to drill when in presence of the foe."

As to the ongoing concern over financial support of the mission, Hudson wrote:

"I need not remind you of the liberal help which the Lord has sent us direct, in our time of need, from certain donors, nor of the blessed fact that He abideth faithful and cannot deny Himself. If we are really trusting in Him and seeking from Him, we cannot be put to shame. If not, perhaps the sooner we find out the unsoundness of any other foundation, the better. The Mission funds, or the donors, are a poor substitute for the living God."

Early in 1871 Hudson's liver ailment grew worse. His lungs caused not just pain, but serious difficulty in breathing. And the resulting sleepless nights caused a physical breakdown and spiritual discouragement. There seemed no alternative but to journey home to recover his health and see to mission business back in England.

Hudson had no idea what desert-dry times lay ahead or how much he had yet to learn about Jesus' promise to always quench the thirst of the thirsty.

17

---

*"My path is far from easy. I never was more
happy in Jesus, and I am very sure He
will not fail us; but never from the
foundation of the mission have we been
more cast upon God."*

1870 - 1873

In that eventful year of 1870, Hudson Taylor was still a young man in his thirties. The China Inland Mission included thirty-three members and occupied stations in three of China's twelve provinces. And all its Chinese converts were gathered into a dozen small congregations.

Yet after sixteen years of demanding, health-breaking missionary service at great personal cost (the loss of his wife and three of his beloved children), Hudson hadn't lost sight of the goal. In fact he felt more certain than ever that God had called, and was still calling, him to evangelize the whole country of China—as impossibly huge as the task seemed.

So it was a physically worn and weary man, but by no means a defeated one, who finally accepted the inevitable need to journey once again to England to regain his health—and of course to do whatever he could in the way of mission business while he was there.

Miss Jenny Faulding, the youngest of the missionaries to accompany the Taylors on the *Lammermuir* and the one who had done such an impressive job heading up the women's work in Hang-chow, had been due to go on furlough and had attempted to purchase passage on an earlier ship. When those plans fell through she happened to be taking the same steamer Hudson took to England. During the two-month voyage, Hudson found the respect and brotherly fondness he had always felt toward Jenny quickly developing into more than friendship. And not long after they reached England, Hudson and Jenny were married.

But despite this new cause for joy in his life, and his quickly returning health, the furlough, designed as a time of rejuvenation, instead brought a greater level of new responsibility and added work than Hudson had imagined—more, it soon proved, than he could ever hope to handle.

By the end of 1871, it became clear that Mr. and Mrs. Berger, who had so generously cared for the home side of the mission, could no longer continue their strenuous labors. Failing health required them to spend winter abroad. Saint Hill, the beautiful home they so generously allowed to serve as the home headquarters of the China Inland Mission, needed to be sold. Now all correspondence, account-keeping, editorial work, screening and testing of candidates, and day-to-day management of the mission's business had to be assumed by someone else. That someone was Hudson.

There was no one else besides Mr. Berger who knew enough about the ongoing operation of the mission to step in. Hudson would have to stay in England until other arrangements could be made. And an impatient, discouraged Hudson Taylor realized that he had no idea what those arrangements should be or how long they would take.

More than ever before he felt the call of China and that great country's spiritual needs. But now, in addition to his seemingly impossible responsibilities as director of the mission in China itself, he was suddenly the mission's sole executive in charge of the home office.

It wasn't much of an office. From the beautiful setting of Saint Hill, the China Inland Mission's headquarters had to be moved to Pyrland Road, a little suburban street in the north of London. And the change from Mr. Berger's spacious library to the small back room which served as Hudson's personal study as well as mission headquarters was just as extreme.

During this time, which must have seemed like an interval of serious setback for the mission and for him personally, Hudson wrote:

"My path is far from easy. I never was more happy in Jesus, and I am very sure He will not fail us; but never from the foundation of the mission have we been more cast upon God. It is well, doubtless, that it should be so. Difficulties afford a platform upon which He can show Himself. Without them we could never know how tender, faithful, and almighty our God is . . . The change about Mr. and Mrs. Berger has tried me not a little. I love them so dearly! And it seems another link severed with the past in which my precious departed one, who is seldom absent from my thoughts, had a part. But His word is, 'Behold, I make all things new.' "

After years of challenging, exciting work in China, it must have been difficult indeed for Hudson to yield to the routine of office work as weeks and months went by. Yet he found contentment enough to write one of his fellow missionaries:

"It is no small comfort to me to know that God has called me to my work, putting me where I am and as I am. I have not sought the position and I dare not leave it. He knows why He places me here—whether to do, or learn, or suffer. 'He that believeth shall not make haste.' That is no easy lesson for you or me; but I honestly think that ten years would be well spent, and we should have our full value for them, if we thoroughly learned it in them . . . Moses seems to have been taken aside for forty years to learn it . . . Meanwhile, let us beware alike of the haste of the impatient, impetuous flesh, and of its disappointment and weariness."

It certainly wasn't as if nothing was being accomplished. Hudson made many new friends and contacts for the mission. Numerous churches and groups asked him to speak to them about his experience and work. And his witness and example attracted many young people to consider missionary service in China.

F. W. Baller, for example, was one young man who went on to become not only a pioneer missionary in China, but a noted linguist and scholar of the Chinese language. At this time, however, he was merely a bright young Londoner who had recently become a Christian and was curious about what it would mean to become a missionary. One day he made his way to Pyrland Road where he found himself in a plainly furnished room in which a small group of people were gathering for a prayer meeting. He later recalled:

"A large text faced the door by which we entered, 'My God shall supply all your need,' and—as I was not accustomed to seeing texts hung on walls in that way— decidedly impressed me. Between a dozen and twenty people were present . . .

"Mr. Taylor, opening the meeting by giving out a hymn and seating himself at the harmonium, led the singing. His appearance did not impress me. He was slightly built, and spoke in a quiet voice. Like most young men, I suppose I associated power with noise, and looked for a physical presence in a leader. But when he said, 'Let us pray,' and proceeded to lead the meeting in prayer, my ideas underwent a change. I had never heard anyone pray like that. There was a simplicity, a tenderness, a boldness, a power that hushed and subdued me, and made it clear that God had admitted him to the inner circle of His friendship. Such praying was evidently the outcome of long tarrying in the secret place, and was a dew from the Lord.

"I have heard many men pray in public since then, but the prayers of Mr. Taylor and the prayers of Mr. Spurgeon stand all by themselves. Who that heard could ever forget them? It was the experience of a lifetime to hear Mr. Spurgeon pray, taking as it were the great congregation of six thousand people by the hand and leading them into the holy place. And to hear Mr. Taylor plead for China was to know something of what is meant by 'the effectual fervent prayer of a righteous man.' That meeting lasted from four to six o'clock, but seemed one of the shortest prayer meetings I had ever attended."

From the west of England, a young woman of education and refinement, Miss Soltau, had come to London to attend the Mildmay Conference, a large Christian meeting held near the China Inland Mission headquarters. While at the conference she stayed as a guest at Pyrland Road. She heard Mr. Taylor give the opening address of the conference, when two to three thousand people crowded the great hall, and saw how he influenced leaders of Christian thought. But it was in the everyday life of the mission house that Hudson Taylor most impressed her and was a big part of the inspiration that led her also into missionary service in China. Long afterwards she wrote of those first days in London:

"I remember Mr. Taylor's exhortation to keep silent to all around and let our wants be known to God only. One day when we had had a small breakfast and there was scarcely anything for dinner, I was thrilled to hear him singing the Children's hymn: 'Jesus loves me, this I know, For the Bible tells me so.'

"Then he called us together to praise the Lord for His changeless love, to tell our needs and claim the promises. And before the day was over we were rejoicing in His gracious answers."

Far from being disheartened by the shortness of funds after Mr. Berger's retirement, Hudson determined to press forward with the mission's goal. Standing before the big map of China one day in the office at Pyrland Road, he turned to a few friends who were with him and asked: "Have you faith to join me in laying hold upon God for eighteen men to go two and two to the nine unevangelised provinces?" And the little group joined hands in front of the map to pray and promise each other and God that they would each continue to pray every day for the eighteen evangelists needed to meet the new goal.

As the months in England passed, a very promising solution was found to the problem of home leadership of the mission. Instead of one person like Mr. Berger who would devote most of his time and service to the task, Hudson established a council of Christian friends who were willing and able to divide among themselves the home work of the mission. The work could go on without unduly overloading anyone on the council. And Hudson and his new bride could finally go back to the front lines of the work in China.

Emily Blatchley would remain with the Taylor children at Pyrland Road. Being intimately acquainted with the mission's work in China and at home (as a result of her former role as Hudson's personal secretary), she could provide invaluable assistance to the council as well. She would keep up the regular weekly prayer meetings at mission headquarters and provide a center there in London for returning missionaries. She would attend to daily business and correspondence while passing along any letters the council needed to handle. The council would be responsible for interviewing candidates, dispensing funds, and keeping friends of the mission appraised of its work through the continuing publication of the "Occasional Paper."

Though confident that business at home was again in good hands as they left once more for China, funds were still low. The mission's bank account was a paltry twenty-one pounds when the Taylors set sail. But there was no debt. And Hudson was able to write in a letter to friends of the mission:

"Now that the work has grown, more helpers are needed at home, as abroad, but the principles of action remain the same. We shall seek pecuniary aid from God by prayer, as heretofore. He will put it into the hearts of those He sees fit to use to act as His channels. When there is money in hand it will be remitted to China; when there is none, none will be sent; and we shall not draw upon home, so that there can be no going into debt. Should our faith be tried as it has been before, the Lord will prove Himself faithful as He has ever done. Nay, should our faith fail, His faithfulness will not—for it is written, 'If we believe not, yet he abideth faithful.' "

Never had Hudson needed that confidence more than when, after an absence of fifteen months, he once again reached China. Sickness and other problems had discouraged missionaries in several of the older, more established centers. (Hudson's old friend George Duncan had left Nanking due to illness and was even then on his way back to England to die.) Even the little Chinese churches had dwindled; many stations were undermanned, some had been closed. So much help and encouragement was needed that Hudson hardly knew where to begin. Instead of planning for an advance to unreached provinces, it looked like a major task just to build up the existing work to its previous level.

In wintry weather, the snow deep on the ground, Hudson left his wife to attend to the work in Hang-chow and set off up the Grand Canal to Chin-kiang. It must have seemed especially lonely to open up the empty mission house that had been such a happy home to his family. From there he wrote his wife to say:

"I have invited the church members and inquirers to dine with me tomorrow [Sunday]. I want them all to meet together. May the Lord give us His blessing. Though things are sadly discouraging, they are not hopeless; they will soon look up, by God's blessing, if they are looked after."

That was his attitude everywhere he went. Finally he was joined by his wife in Nanking where together they spent three months working in direct evangelism. From there he reported back home:

"Every night we gather large numbers by means of pictures and lantern slides and preach to them Jesus . . . We had fully five hundred in the chapel last night. Some did not stay long; others were there nearly three hours. May the Lord bless our stay here to souls . . . Every afternoon women come to see and hear."

Evidence of his great inner strength was seen in a letter he wrote to Emily Blatchley in which he asked: "If you are ever drinking at the Fountain with what will your life be running over?—Jesus, Jesus, Jesus!"

It was a full cup of faith Hudson Taylor carried. And the overflow of that spirit proved to be just what was needed by the mission in China. His visits accomplished their objective of encouragement and were continued until he had been, at least once, to every station and almost every outstation in the mission. And his concern was not just for his fellow missionaries. Everywhere he went he sought out the Chinese Christians to help and encourage them as well.

When they could be together, his wife's assistance was invaluable; they would work at times far into the night attending to correspondence. On medical journeys she was often his companion; or she might remain at one station where there was sickness, while he went on to another. Repeatedly, they felt grateful for his medical knowledge, for there was no other doctor in the mission or anywhere away from the treaty ports in those years.

Of course, his medical expertise often added to his burden of work. For example, Hudson once reached a distant station to find ninety-eight letters awaiting him. Yet the very next day he took time to write a full page of medical instructions about "A-liang's baby." (A-liang was one of the valued Chinese helpers at Chin-kiang.) But whether it meant longer letters or extra journeys, Hudson thanked God for any and every way in which he could help. Because it was, as he said and showed many times, his greatest desire to be "servant of all."

After being back in China about nine months, Hudson wrote:

"The Lord is prospering us and the work is steadily growing, especially in that most important department, native help. The helpers themselves need much help, much care and instruction; but they are becoming more efficient as well as more numerous, and the hope for China lies doubtless in them. I look on foreign missionaries as the scaffolding round a rising building; the sooner it can be dispensed with the better—or the sooner, rather, that it can be transferred to serve the same temporary purpose elsewhere."

Winter came again. Yet the seasons seldom changed the number of demands on Hudson's time. In the coldest of weather he continued on the road. After ten out of twelve weeks spent away from his wife, the two of them finally managed to meet at an empty mission house in Feng-hwa where they enjoyed being together alone, truly alone, for the first time since they had been married.

Their little honeymoon soon ended with a call for help from the Crombies whose only remaining children were on the verge of death. So Hudson set off on a two-day journey over mountain passes drifted high with snow. By the time he could return from there, another message arrived from an even more distant station saying an entire family had come down with smallpox. Waiting only until his coolie arrived with his belongings (Hudson had raced ahead to rejoin his wife), he set out again across the mountains on treacherously icy trails that were sometimes nothing more than steps carved out of rock.

In the stress and strain of just keeping the mission going, it would have been easy to forget about his dream of expanding the ministry, especially when funds for the current work were none too plentiful. But Hudson couldn't forget. Traveling from place to place on long journeys between the stations through populous country teeming with friendly, accessible people, his heart went out more and more to the unreached, both near and far. He wrote to the council in London:

"Last week I was at Taiping. My heart was greatly moved by the crowds that literally filled the streets for two or three miles, so that we could hardly walk, for it was market day. We did but little preaching, for we were looking for a place for permanent work, but I was constrained to retire to the city wall and cry to God to have mercy on the people, to open their hearts and give us an entrance among them.

"Without any seeking on our part, we were brought into touch with at least four anxious souls. An old man found us out, I know not how, and followed me to our boat. I asked him in and inquired his name.

" 'My name is Dzing,' he replied. 'But the question which distresses me, and to which I can find no answer, is—What am I to do with my sins? Our scholars tell us that there is no future state, but I find it hard to believe them . . . Oh, sir, I lie on my bed and think. I sit alone in the daytime and think. I think and think and think again, but I cannot tell what is to be done about my sins. I am seventy-two years of age. I cannot expect to finish another decade. "Today knows not tomorrow's lot," as the saying is. Can you tell me what to do with my sins?'

" 'I can indeed,' was my reply. 'It is to answer this very question that we have come so many thousands of miles. Listen, and I will explain to you what you want and need to know.'

"When my companions returned, he heard again the wonderful story of the Cross, and left us soothed and comforted . . . glad to know that we had rented a house and hoped soon to have Chinese Christians distributing Bibles and Christian literature in that city."

So moved was Hudson by encountering that kind of spiritual hunger that the next day he wrote in his Bible:

"Asked God for fifty or a hundred additional native evangelists and as many missionaries as may be needed to open up the four Fu's and forty-eight Hsien cities still unoccupied in Che-kiang, also for men to break into the nine unoccupied provinces. Asked in the name of Jesus.

"I thank Thee, Lord Jesus, for the promise whereon Thou hast given me to rest. Give me all needed strength of body, wisdom of mind, grace of soul to do this Thy so great work."

What followed that prayer wasn't renewed strength, but another bout of serious illness. Week after week he lay in bed suffering helplessly with hardly more than enough energy to pray. Funds had been so low for months that he hardly knew how to distribute the little that came in. There certainly was nothing with which to begin expanding the work. Still "we are going on to the interior," he had written to the secretaries in London. "I do so hope to see some of the destitute provinces evangelised before long. I long for it by day and pray for it by night. Can He care less?"

Never had advance seemed more impossible. But in his Bible was the record of his prayer, and in his heart was the conviction that, even for inland China, God's time had almost come. It was then, while he was still in bed recovering, that he received a letter from England written two months before by a woman he had never met. Her trembling hand had written:

"My dear sir, I bless God—in two months I hope to place at the disposal of your Council, for further extension of the China Inland Mission work, eight hundred pounds. Please remember, for fresh provinces . . .

"I think your receipt form beautiful: 'The Lord our Banner; The Lord will provide.' If faith is put before and praise sent up, I am sure that Jehovah of Hosts will honour it."

Spiritual Secret   219

Eight hundred pounds for "fresh provinces"! Even before he recorded his prayer in his Bible, the letter had been sent and God had been answering his request. Surely, he thought, the time for advancing the work had come.

But Hudson couldn't see the dark days that still lay ahead.

18

"After living on God's faithfulness for many years, I can testify that times of want have ever been times of special blessing, or have led to them. I do beg that never any appeal for funds be put forward, save to God in prayer. When our work becomes a begging work, it dies. God is faithful, must be so."

1872 - 1876

Hudson was so encouraged by the answer to his prayer that he soon recovered enough to travel back to the Yangtze valley to find spring weather and a warm new enthusiasm spreading throughout the mission. In Chin-kiang, as in almost all the stations, Chinese Christians seemed to be growing rapidly in their faith. New converts came to the churches. And Chinese leaders were encouraging and instructing their own people.

Calling as many missionaries as could leave their stations, Hudson convened a special conference in Chin-kiang. All those who came found inspiration in the good reports of their colleagues' progress. And the group joined together in prayer with Hudson before he and Mr. Judd set out up the great river in search of a new base city from which they could move on into the westernmost provinces of China.

Before he left Hudson wrote, "Is it not good of the Lord to encourage us when we are sorely tried from want of funds?"

It certainly wasn't an abundance of supplies that accounted for the heightened enthusiasm within the mission. And it wasn't because everything now seemed to be going Hudson's way either. While in Chin-kiang Hudson had received the surprising and disturbing news that Emily Blatchley had fallen seriously ill back in London. Not only was he saddened to learn that the prospects for her recovery were very slim, but he wondered

Hudson Taylor's

what was to become of the children to whom she had been serving as volunteer mother. And then there was the work of the home office, more and more of which had fallen upon her in his absence. She not only operated the mission house, she took over the editing and distribution of the "Occasional Paper," dealt with much correspondence herself, and conducted the regular prayer meeting on behalf of the mission.

Hudson confided in a letter to a close Christian friend before he left on his longest journey yet up the Yangtze, saying:

"Never has our work entailed such real trial or so much exercise of faith. The sickness of our beloved friend Miss Blatchley, and her strong desire to see me; the needs of our dear children; the state of funds; the changes required in the work to admit of some going home, others coming out, and of further expansion; and many other things not easily expressed in writing, would be crushing burdens if we were to bear them. But the Lord bears us and them too, and makes our hearts so very glad in Himself—not Himself plus a bank balance—that I have never known greater freedom from care and anxiety.

"The other week, when I reached Shanghai, we were in great and immediate need. The mails were both in, but no remittance! And the folios showed no balance at home. I cast the burden on the Lord. Next morning on waking I felt inclined to trouble, but the Lord gave me a word—'I know their sorrows, and am come down to deliver'; 'Certainly I will be with thee'—and before 6 a.m. I was as sure that help was at hand when, near noon, I received a letter from Mr. Muller which had been to Ning-po and thus delayed in reaching me, and which contained more than three hundred pounds.

Spiritual Secret   223

"My need now is great and urgent, but God is greater and more near. And because He is what He is, all must be, all is, all will be well. Oh, my dear brother, the joy of knowing the living God, of seeing the living God, of resting on the living God in our very special and peculiar circumstances! I am but His agent. He will have to look after His own Honour, provide for His own servants, and supply all our need according to His own riches, you helping by your prayers and work of faith and labour of love."

In a note to his wife that spring, Hudson included a sobering report: "The balance in hand yesterday was eighty-seven cents." But to that he added, "The Lord reigns; herein is our joy and rest!" And to Mr. Baller he added, when the balance was still lower, "We have this—and all the promises of God."

"Twenty-five cents," Baller recalled later, "plus all the promises of God! Why, one felt as rich as Croesus!"

Hudson challenged everyone to trust in God's provision. And he wrote numerous letters with the same warning he gave to a council member in the following letter:

"I am truly sorry that you should be distressed at not having funds to send me. May I not say, 'Be careful for nothing.' We should use all care to economise what God does send us; but when that is done bear no care about real or apparent lack. After living on God's faithfulness for many years, I can testify that times of want have ever been times of special blessing, or have led to them. I do beg that never any appeal for funds be put forward, save to God in prayer. When our work becomes a begging work, it dies. God is faithful, must be so. 'The Lord is my Shepherd, I shall not want.' "

Hudson Taylor's

He didn't want anyone connected with the mission to be tempted to help by making financial appeals in meetings or to individuals. So he had chosen the theme of the Chinkiang conference that spring from a hymn: "In some way or another the Lord will provide."

It was with this same theme in mind that Hudson wrote a letter of support and encouragement to Emily Blatchley to let her know that he would be heading back to England as soon as possible. In the letter he said:

"I am sure that, if we but wait, the Lord will provide . . . We go shortly, that is, Mr. Judd and myself, to see if we can procure headquarters at Wuchang, from which to open up western China as the Lord may enable us. We are urged on to make this effort now, though so weak-handed, both by the need of the unreached provinces and by our having funds in hand for work in them, while we have none for general purposes . . . I cannot conceive how we shall be helped through next month, though I fully expect we shall be. The Lord cannot and will not fail us."

Things didn't look much better financially by the time Hudson had returned from Wuchang after getting his friend Mr. Judd established in a new station there. So the Taylors set out once again to England, to see about their friend Emily Blatchley and to do what they could for the mission work at home.

But this homecoming turned out to be a sad one. Emily Blatchley, faithful friend to the end, had died while they were en route. The Taylors found the house at Pyrland Road empty, the children scattered among various friends and relatives, the home work of the mission at a standstill, even the weekly prayer meeting discontinued.

Mission business seemed in as much disarray at home as it had been in China the last time they arrived there. To

Hudson it must have seemed a new all-time low point in the life of his mission. And yet things were about to sink lower still.

• • •

On his trip up the Yangtze to reach Wuchang, Hudson had slipped on the gangway of a small cargo boat and fallen hard, spraining an ankle and wrenching his back. Though he was disabled a few days at the time, he was eventually able to walk and endure the resulting pain.

But now, within a week or two of his return to London, he began to feel a numbness in his limbs. His doctor diagnosed the problem as a "concussion of the spine" and ordered absolute and complete bed rest. Even then he offered only faint hope Hudson would ever be able to stand or walk again.

Hudson had no choice but to lie in his upstairs room, conscious of all there was to be done for the mission—all that could not be attended to. He had been halfway around the world and back three times, had seen more of China than any European since Marco Polo, and was still clinging to the vision that God wanted him to take the gospel to all the unreached provinces of that land. Yet here he lay, his personal realm suddenly limited to a narrow four-poster bed. But on the wall at the foot of his bed, where he could see it always between the posts, hung Hudson's big map of China.

Years later a church leader from Scotland said to Hudson, "You must sometimes be tempted to be proud because of the wonderful way God has used you. I doubt if any man living has had greater honour."

"On the contrary," Hudson replied. "I often think that God must have been looking for someone small enough and weak enough for Him to use, and that He found me."

For it was indeed in Hudson's weakness that God began to work in a mighty way.

The outlook did not brighten as the year drew to a close. Hudson's paralysis progressed; he was less and less able to move and could only turn in bed with the help of a rope fixed above him. At first he had managed to write a little, but now he could not even hold a pen. It was then, with the dawn of 1875, that the Christian press printed a little paper he had written titled, "Appeal for Prayer: on behalf of more than a hundred and fifty millions of Chinese." Briefly it stated the facts with regard to the nine unevangelized provinces and the aims of the mission. Four thousand pounds, it said, had recently been given for the special purpose of sending the gospel to these distant regions. Chinese Christians were ready to take part in the work. The urgent need was for more missionaries, young men willing to face any hardship in leading the way.

"Will each of your Christian readers," the article requested, "at once raise his heart to God, spending one minute in earnest prayer that God will raise up, this year, eighteen suitable men to devote themselves to this work?"

The article didn't say that the leader of the mission was, to all appearances, a hopeless invalid. It did not refer to the fact that the four thousand pounds had come from Hudson and his wife. (It was part of their capital from her recent inheritance. They were already donating all the interest from the capital to the work of the mission.) Neither did the article mention the covenant of two or three years previously, when Hudson and a few friends determined to pray daily in faith for the eighteen evangelists until they should be given. And yet many who read the article were moved by its challenge.

Before long, Hudson's correspondence began to increase. So did his joy and confidence in dealing with it—or rather, seeing how the Lord dealt with it. He wrote of this time:

"The Mission had no paid helpers, but God led volunteers, without pre-arrangement, to come in from day to day, to write from dictation. If one who called in the morning could not stay long enough to answer all letters, another was sure to come, and perhaps one or two might look in, in the afternoon. Occasionally a young friend employed in the city would come in after business hours and do needful bookkeeping, or finish letters not already dealt with. So it was day by day. One of the happiest periods of my life was that period of inactivity, when one could do nothing but rejoice in the Lord and 'wait patiently' for Him, and see Him meeting all one's need. Never were my letters, before or since, kept so regularly and promptly answered.

"And the eighteen asked of God began to come. There was some first correspondence, then they came to see me in my room. Soon I had a class studying Chinese at my bedside. In due time the Lord sent them all forth; and then dear friends at Mildmay [the nearby Christian conference center] began to pray for my restoration. The Lord blessed the means used, and I was risen up. One reason for my being laid aside was gone. Had I been well and able to move about, some might have thought that my urgent appeals, rather than God's working, had sent the eighteen men to China. But utterly laid aside, able only to dictate a request for prayer, the answer to our prayers was the more apparent."

One of those who came during this time was the Rev. C. G. Moore, a candidate and eventually a member of the mission serving in China. He wrote this about his first meeting with Hudson Taylor at Pyrland Road:

"[His study] was the back room on the ground floor, and could be entered from the front sitting-room by large folding doors. Shall I say I was shocked or surprised, or both? At any rate I had an absolutely novel experience. The room was largely occupied with packing-cases and some rough shelves set along one of the walls. Near the window, which looked out on the dreary back-gardens, was a writing table littered with papers. In front of the fireplace where a fender is usually found was a low, narrow iron bedstead, neatly covered with a rug—Mr. Taylor's chief resting place by night and by day. I hardly think there was a scrap of carpet on the floor, and certainly not a single piece of furniture that suggested the slightest regard for comfort or appearance.

"Mr. Taylor offered no word of apology or explanation, but lay down on his iron bedstead and eagerly plunged into a conversation, which was, for me, one of life's golden moments. Every idea I had hitherto cherished of a 'great man' was completely shattered: the high, imposing airs, and all the trappings were conspicuously absent; but Christ's ideal of greatness was then and there so securely set in my heart, that it has remained through all the years, up to this moment. I strongly suspect that, by his unconscious influence, Mr. Hudson Taylor did more than any other man of his day to compel Christian people to revise their ideas of greatness . . .

"I mention these details because they throw light upon some of the important principles upon which Mr. Taylor based his life and service. He profoundly realised that if the millions of China were to be evangelised, there would have to be a vast increase in self-denial and self-sacrifice upon the part of Christians at home. But how could he ask and urge others to do what he was not practising himself? So he deliberately stripped his life, on all sides, of every appearance of self-consideration and self-indulgence . . .

"And it was just the same in China; but there an additional principle came into action. He would not ask those who worked with him to face hardships he himself was not willing to endure. He never used his position as Director of the Mission to purchase himself the least advantage or ease. He made it his, under all circumstances, to live in that spirit and practise of self-sacrifice which he expected to find in his brethren on the field. However hard his lot might be in China, every missionary knew that Mr. Taylor had suffered in the same way, and was ready to do so again. No man could suspect, at any time, that while he himself was bearing the cross, his leader, under more favourable circumstances, was shirking it. Herein was one explanation of the remarkable and affectionate attachment to Mr. Taylor on the part of so many in the Mission."

But just as the friends and candidates of the mission were challenged by Hudson Taylor's example, they also learned to trust the power of prayer. The monthly remittance to be cabled to China on one occasion was very small, nearly £235 less than the average expenditure to be covered. So when the household gathered for noon prayers, Hudson suggested: "Let us bring the matter to the Lord in prayer." That very evening the postman brought a letter which was found to contain a check to be entered, "From the sale of plate"—and the sum was just over £235.

Once, after he was able to be up and about again, Hudson was returning from a meeting when he happened to take a seat on a train beside a Russian nobleman who had heard him speak at the meeting. As they traveled to

London together, Count Bobrinsky took out his pocketbook.

"Allow me to give you a trifle," he said, "toward your work in China."

But the banknote he handed to Mr. Taylor was a large sum. Hudson realized that there must have been some mistake. "Did you not mean to give me five pounds?" he asked. "Please let me return this note, it is for fifty!"

"I cannot take it back," replied the Count who was just as surprised as Hudson. "Five pounds was what I meant to give, but God must have intended you to have fifty. I cannot take it back."

Impressed with what had taken place, Hudson reached Pyrland Road to find family and friends gathered for special prayer. A China remittance was to be sent out, and the money in hand was short by forty-nine pounds, eleven shillings. There on the table Hudson laid his banknote for fifty pounds.

But even after all the answers to prayer in those years, enormous barriers still remained. In fact, in the months immediately after the eighteen pioneer missionaries sailed from England for China, the two countries again came to the brink of war.

A British official traveling into far western China was murdered. When the government in London lodged a protest, the Chinese government ignored the demands. The British ambassador, having exhausted all diplomatic channels, left Peking for the coast to sail home. War looked inevitable at the very time Hudson was preparing to follow the eighteen new missionaries to China, accompanied by yet another eight new workers.

Many friends of the mission tried to talk Hudson out of going. "You will all have to return," they said. "And as to sending off pioneers to the more distant provinces, it is simply out of the question."

But Hudson felt certain that there had been no mistake. The men and money were finally available. Certainly the time had come to take the gospel where it had never been before. Was inland China going to remain closed?

Hudson spent many long hours on his knees in the third-class cabin of the French steamer that carried the Taylors and their eight new young colleagues toward China. Two years before he had written, "My soul yearns, oh how intensely, for the evangelisation of the hundred and eighty millions of these unoccupied provinces. Oh, that I had a hundred lives to give or spend for their good!" In the meantime he did everything in his power, and more, to keep that vision alive. He and the mission had gone through so much. And now . . . ?

At the last moment the Chinese government relented. The Viceroy, Li Hung-chang, rushed to the coast, overtaking the British Minister at Chefoo. And it was there that the memorable convention was signed which finally promised complete access to every part of China.

When Hudson reached Shanghai the good news awaited him. The agreement had been signed the week after he sailed from England. And three parties of the Eighteen had already set out and were well on their way into the interior.

"Just as our brethren were ready," Hudson wrote, "not too soon and not too late, the long-closed door opened to them of its own accord."

19

"It is difficult to realise that I cannot run about as I once did . . . [But] the weakness that prevents overwork may be the greatest blessing to me."

1876 - 1881

While the doors to inland China were technically "open" for some years, they were only open a crack. But the Chefoo Convention, in effect, flung wide the doors. The agreement not only stated that foreigners were at liberty to travel anywhere in the Emperor's dominions (earlier agreements had promised that), but this time foreign travelers went with the guarantee of the Emperor's own protection and were to be received with respect and in no way hindered in their journey. Imperial proclamations declaring this policy were to be posted in every city. And for a period of two years, British officials could be sent anywhere in China to make sure all these provisions were carried out.

The China Inland Mission representatives were the first, and in many parts of China, the only foreigners to make use of this opportunity. And on more than one occasion alarmed local government officials would welcome the unexpected missionaries to a new city with elaborate hospitality, while their minions hurriedly tacked up the official documents they were supposed to have posted.

Far and wide the pioneer missionaries traveled—crossing and recrossing all the provinces of the interior and penetrating even into Tibet. Over thirty thousand miles those men journeyed in the first eighteen months.

The way, however, wasn't at all easy. For while the Chinese government approved their travel, many leaders still resented the presence of westerners. And the rigors of travel, mostly on foot or by wheelbarrow, remained as difficult as ever.

Hudson himself was able to accomplish little of what he planned in the first few months back in China. A fever he caught while sailing up the China Sea led to a serious illness that confined him for some time in Chin-kiang where he could do little except pray and help with mission correspondence.

"It is difficult to realise that I cannot run about as I once did," he wrote to his wife. Jenny had stayed in England to care for the Taylor children, the older four, two little ones born to her, and the adopted orphan daughter of George Duncan. And in a later letter he added, "The weakness that prevents overwork may be the greatest blessing to me."

But overwork could hardly be avoided. In addition to his responsibilities as director of all the work in China, and the editing of *China's Millions*, a new illustrated magazine the mission published and sold back in England, Hudson soon took over the office duties of the mission secretary whose health forced him to go home on furlough.

Whenever work permitted, Hudson liked to take a break to play the harmonium and sing hymns. His favorite contained the words:

"Jesus, I am resting, resting, in the joy of what Thou art; I am finding out the greatness of Thy loving heart."

One of the eighteen pioneer evangelists, Mr. George Nichols, was with Hudson on one occasion when the mail arrived in the office with the disturbing news of serious rioting around two of the older stations of the mission.

Thinking Hudson might wish to be alone, the younger man was about to withdraw when, to his surprise, Hudson began to whistle that same refrain—"Jesus, I am resting, resting, in the joy of what Thou art . . ."

Turning in surprise, George Nichols exclaimed, "How can you whistle, when our friends are in so much danger!"

"Would you have me anxious and troubled?" Hudson responded. "That would not help them, and would certainly incapacitate me for my work. I have just to roll the burden on the Lord."

Day and night that was what he did. Frequently anyone awake in the little mission house at Chin-kiang might hear, at 2 a.m. or 3 a.m., the soft refrain of Hudson's favorite hymn which spelled out his strategy for handling all the pressures and problems the mission faced.

By the time Hudson regained strength enough to travel he knew he would need to stay longer in China than the forty weeks he originally planned. "Sometimes it does seem hard," he wrote Jenny, "to be away from you. But when I think of the One Who spent 33 years away from His heaven, and finished them on Calvary, I feel ashamed of my own selfishness."

Though Hudson and Jenny enjoyed a wonderful reunion when he returned after sixteen months in China, their time together was short. For Hudson brought with him the dreadful news of a famine in North China where six million Chinese faced starvation after several straight years of lost crops. The two pioneer missionaries recently sent to that region reported that children were dying by the thousands and young girls were being sold into slavery and taken away in large numbers to be resold in southern Chinese cities.

Hudson felt so burdened by the conditions in North

China that he devoted most of his energies to telling Christians throughout Britain about the needed relief work. But when funds began coming in for the rescue of starving children, the next problem became obvious.

Where was the woman who could go to that province to head up the relief work among the women and children? No European woman had ever been beyond the mountains that separated Shansi from the coast. Just to get there meant a journey of two weeks by mule-litter, over dangerous roads, with miserable inns at night.

Experienced, devoted, with a knowledge of the language, and having already earned the confidence of fellow missionaries, both men and women, Jenny Taylor couldn't help thinking she was the person who needed to go. But how could she? She and Hudson had just been separated for more than a year. He, as usual, had worn himself out in China and could use her help with mission business at home. And who would care for the seven children?

As she struggled with the decision, Jenny prayed that God would give her a sign. "I felt like Gideon," she wrote, "that my strength in China would be 'Have not I commanded thee?' and I wanted some fleeces to confirm my faith, and as a token for those who would have me remain at home. I asked God to give me, in the first place, money to purchase certain requisites for outfit, as we had none to spare; and further, to give me liberally, as much as fifty pounds, so that there might be money in hand when I went away."

The very next day a friend called to see her, saying, "Will you accept a little gift for your own use, to get anything you need for the journey?" And the gift was ten pounds, exactly the allowance the mission made for outfitting a missionary for the trip to China. A few days later she received another unexpected check, for exactly fifty pounds. Her fleeces so precisely answered, she knew what she must do.

And, finally, the solution to her greatest concern was also provided when Hudson's sister, Amelia Broomhall, who lived next door to the Pyrland Road headquarters, announced, "If Jenny is called to go to China, I am called to care for her children."

So for another year Hudson and Jenny were separated. While she ministered to the needs of starving women and children in North China, he oversaw the training of yet another thirty new missionaries and began to see a new complication resulting from the expansion of the mission.

The pioneer missionaries naturally sought headquarters where they could establish their own homes. And just as naturally, many decided to get married. That meant sending women into the vast interior of China—something no other mission had ever done—and immediately prompted a new wave of criticism about the China Inland Mission's policies. Married couples would soon have children and single women would then need to be sent to help take over some of the busy mothers' duties of evangelism and teaching among the Chinese women. And if he thought the criticism for sending married women out into pioneer missionary work was severe, it was nothing compared to the outcry over allowing single women to be exposed to the dangers and hardships of life in inland China.

But Hudson, having seen the great effectiveness of Maria during his early days in China, and now having sent Jenny on her unprecedented assignment into Shansi, had great confidence in the courage, strength, and resourcefulness of women missionaries. So by the time he and Jenny were reunited in Shanghai in 1879 for an extended tour of the mission centers around China, the decision to open up "women's work" was already made. And it soon turned out to be one of the most significant decisions Hudson ever made.

Stranded for a time in the Yangtze gorges, the first women who went to the far west spent a strange Christmas amid their belongings spread out to dry upon the rocks. And what crowds overwhelmed them when they reached their destinations!

"For nearly two months past," Mrs. Nichols wrote from Chungking, "I have seen some hundreds of women daily. Our house has been like a fair."

More than once she fainted from exhaustion in the midst of a crowd of guests who came to sit and listen to the gospel story told by the only white woman in a province of some sixty million people. And when she returned to consciousness she would find the women fanning her, full of affection and concern. One lady, who cared for her like a mother, would send round her own sedan chair with an urgent request for Mrs. Nichols to return in it immediately. The most comfortable bed in her apartment was waiting, and after sending out all the younger women she would sit down herself to fan the weary visitor till she fell asleep. Then an inviting dinner was prepared, and on no account was Mrs. Nichols allowed to leave until she ate a healthy meal.

Everywhere those first women went, they were surprised at how glad the people were to see them, how eager they were to hear their message. And not just out of curiosity, but with genuine interest in the Bible and in this man Jesus. So that by the end of the second year after missionary women came on the scene, the pioneers were rejoicing in sixty or seventy converts gathered into little churches in the far inland provinces.

But no one knew the cost and the danger of such work any better than Hudson Taylor. Having lost his beloved Maria to the demands and disease of China, he prayed every day for the health and safety of every woman in the mission. But, as he wrote his mother:

"I cannot tell you how glad my heart is to see the work extending and consolidating in the remote parts of China. It is worth living for and worth dying for."

Indeed he almost did die. It was a great blessing that Jenny was with him in China because his life was threatened by illness three times during 1879. Her supportive, inspiring attitude can be seen in a letter written at the time which said:

"Don't you think that if we set ourselves not to allow any pressure to rob us of communion with the Lord, we may live lives of hourly triumph, the echo for which will come back to us from every part of the Mission? I have been feeling these last months that of all our work the most important is that unseen, upon the mount of intercession. Our faith must gain the victory for the fellow-workers God has given us. They fight the seen and we must fight the unseen battle. And dare we claim less than constant victory, when it is for Him, and we come in His Name?"

Though Hudson did pull through and began to regain his strength, his trial regarding finances continued. "Funds seem to be dropping lower and lower. We need much prayer. But God cannot fail us; let us trust and not be afraid," he wrote to a fellow missionary.

And when another friend noted how much of his convalescence seemed to be spent in prayer, Hudson asked

"What would you do if you had a large family and nothing to give them to eat? That is almost my situation at present."

When word reached China that both of their mothers had died within a few weeks of each other, Hudson and Jenny decided she was needed at home. He would follow as soon as possible.

His wife had only been gone ten days when he wrote:

"I am sure you have been longing for me, as I for you. At the right time, by the right way, the Lord will bring us together again. Let us seek to live all the more with Him, to find Him a satisfying portion."

And a month later, as he journeyed up the Yangtze, he wrote:

"You are ploughing the Mediterranean and will soon see Naples . . . I am waiting for a steamer to Wuchang. I need not, cannot tell you how much I miss you, but God is making me feel how rich we are in His presence and love . . . He is helping me to rejoice in our adverse circumstances, in our poverty, in the retirements from our Mission. All these difficulties are only platforms for the manifestations of His grace, power, and love.

"I am very busy [he continued from Wuchang when his meetings there had begun]. God is giving us a happy time of fellowship together, and is confirming us in the principles on which we are acting."

That last statement was a crucial declaration of confidence for the time. Hudson, along with all the other missionaries who gathered at Wuchang, had recommitted themselves to continuing the current course of the mission. And the mission was fast approaching another point of crisis.

After years of prayer, patience, and persevering effort, a position of unparalleled opportunity had been reached.

Inland China lay open before them. But reinforcements were needed at all the settled stations in the far north, south, and west. Not to advance would be to retreat from the position of faith taken up at the beginning. Not advancing would mean surrendering to difficulties rather than trusting the living God.

True, funds were low, and had been for years. It was also true that the new workers coming out to China were few. So it would have been easy to say, "For the present, no further extension is possible." But not to move forward would mean throwing away the new opportunities God had given. And the feeling among the missionaries was that pulling back could not be God's way for the evangelization of inland China.

So the members of the China Inland Mission instead took a bold and startling step of faith. They agreed, and then sent home word of their agreement, to pray for seventy new workers to come to China. At a time when the entire membership of the mission totaled only a little more than a hundred workers, when funds for their own support were greatly strained, the missionaries agreed to pray for seventy more. Since it didn't seem practical to receive and arrange for so many new workers in a shorter time, they set a three year time-frame on the expansion.

As the conference came to agreement on the matter, someone exclaimed, "If only we could meet again and have a united praise meeting, when the last of the Seventy have reached China!"

"We shall be widely scattered then," said another missionary. "But why not have the praise meeting now? Why not give thanks for the Seventy before we separate?" So they held another prayer service—this time to give thanks in advance for God's answer to their request.

But despite this great display of faith, there were many people back in England, friends and critics alike, who doubted that it could ever happen.

20

---

*"Flesh and heart often fail: let them fail!
He faileth not. Pray very much, pray
constantly, for Satan rages against us . . .
There is much to distress."*

1882 - 1888

In faith, Hudson and his fellow missionaries waited for encouraging word and added support from home. But instead of having their faith rewarded with new and greater resources for advancing into new territory, the existing work of the mission suffered a greater shortage of funds than ever. In October, 1882, he wrote:

"We were at table when we received our letters (the home mail); and when on opening one of them I found, instead of seven or eight hundred pounds for the month's supplies, only [just over] 96 pounds, my feelings I shall not soon forget.

"I closed the envelope again, and seeking my room, knelt down and spread the letter before the Lord, asking Him what was to be done with less than 97 pounds—a sum it was impossible to distribute over seventy stations in which were eighty or ninety missionaries, including their wives, not to speak of about a hundred native helpers, and more than that number of native children to be fed and clothed in our schools. Having first rolled the burden on the Lord, I then mentioned the matter to others of our own Mission in Chefoo, and we unitedly looked to Him to come to our aid; but no hint as to our circumstances was allowed to reach anyone outside.

"Soon the answers began to come—kind gifts from local friends who little knew the peculiar value of their donations, and help in other ways, until the needs of the month were all met without our having been burdened with anxious thoughts even for an hour. We had similar experiences in November and December . . . Thus the Lord made our hearts sing for joy, and provided through local contributions in China for the needs of the work as never before or since."

Experiencing this provision for their current needs, the missionaries felt all the more reassured that God would answer their prayers for the seventy new workers. But realizing the growing doubts back in England, Hudson and his friends gathered for a prayer meeting on the second of February to ask God for some sign that would serve as His stamp of approval and encourage the doubters back home. As Hudson explained:

"We knew that our Father loves to please his children, and we asked him lovingly to please us, as well as to encourage timid ones at home, by leading some one of His wealthy stewards to make room for large blessing for himself and his family by giving liberally to this special object."

It was just a few days later when Hudson sailed for England. So he didn't hear the results of that prayer until his ship stopped at Aden. Though no word of that special prayer meeting had reached home, the home staff at Pyrland Road had been thrilled to receive, on the second of February, an anonymous gift of three thousand pounds. Enclosed with the gift was a verse: "Ask of me, and I shall give thee the heathen for thine inheritance, and the uttermost parts of the earth for my possession."

And that wasn't all. The gift was sent in an unusual way. It was signed from "Father, Mother" and five children. "It was most striking," wrote Hudson, "to see how literally God had answered our prayer, and led his faithful steward to 'make room for a large blessing for himself and his family.' "

And by the time Hudson reached London that spring, he recognized a growing respect for and interest in the work of the China Inland Mission. Word of their pioneering work had begun to spread. Alexander Wylie of the London Missionary Society had written, "They are opening up the country and this is what we want. Other missions are doing a good work, but they are not doing this work."

John McCarthy had just returned on furlough after walking clear across China from east to west, preaching in cities all along the way. Henry Soltau and J. W. Stevenson, the first Europeans to enter western China from Burma had also arrived home to share their experiences. So when Hudson arrived and began making known the appeal for "the Seventy," the Christian community took a new interest in China.

Hudson's brother-in-law, Benjamin Broomhall, had taken over the responsibility of General Secretary of the Home Council and had made many new friends for the mission. So Hudson was invited all over the country to talk about the work. And everywhere he went people were moved as they heard the story of the mission and the ongoing needs of China.

One of the mission's new friends, a minister from Gloucester, said of Hudson's extensive speaking tour:

". . . you could be quite sure that, whatever else he might say, he would make no plea for funds. Often I used to hear him explain, almost apologetically, that his great desire was that no funds should be diverted from other societies to the China Inland Mission; and that it was for this reason he had taken up lines of working which he hoped would preclude interference with other organisations. Nothing gave him more genuine pleasure than to speak well of other missions . . .

"Oh, the self-emptied spirit, the dignified way in which his life of faith was lived out, the reality of it all! Instead of wanting to get anything out of you, he was always ready to give to you. His heart and mind were full of that. Some people seem to be asking all the time, though they may not do so in actual words: he never."

At one conference where he spoke about the needs of China and didn't even mention his own mission's name, even though no collection was taken, the people emptied their purses and stripped off their jewelry to donate it to the cause. And according to one contemporary account, "Fifteen or sixteen offers for the mission field were the result, and a whole jewellery case was sent in the next day. People had received so much that they felt they could give anything."

Even those who had only heard "about" Hudson Taylor responded. One child from Cambridge, to whom "Hudson Taylor" was a household name, wrote saying, "If you are not dead yet, I want to send you the money I have saved up to help the little boys and girls of China to love Jesus."

Canon Wilberforce of Southampton also wrote at this time urging, "Will you do me the kindness to give a Bible-reading in my house to about sixty people . . . and spend the night with us? Please do us this favour, in the Master's name."

And Lord Radstock wrote from the continent saying, "Much love to you in the Lord. You are a great help to us in England by strengthening our faith."

From Dr. Andrew Bonar came one hundred pounds forwarded from an unknown Presbyterian friend "who cares for the land of Sinim." Spurgeon invited him to speak at the Tabernacle, and Miss Macpherson invited him to Bethnal Green.

"My heart is still in the glorious work [wrote Mr. Berger with a check for five hundred pounds]. Most heartily do I join you in praying for seventy more labourers—but I do not stop at seventy! Surely we shall see greater things than these, if we are empty of self, seeking only God's glory and the salvation of souls."

So full was Hudson's time with meetings that it seemed he hardly had time for his directorial duties. And yet one volume, used to note mission correspondence— when received, when answered, and a line about the contents—shows that Hudson personally attended to twenty-six hundred letters in the course of only ten months' time.

There always seemed to be so much work to do. And yet that work was being rewarded. Representatives of the China Inland Mission speaking at Oxford and Cambridge played a major role in the beginning of a student revival which flamed bright and blazed across Britain and eventually to North America. Even at its beginning it inspired so many to consider missionary service that the China Inland Mission was soon flooded with inquiries and enough support that Hudson was able to sail for China to help prepare for the imminent arrival of the last of the Seventy even before the full three-year period was up.

Though heartened to know that the mission and its work had grown popular at home, Hudson knew that the expansion in China would mean even greater challenges.

"Soon we shall be in the midst of the battle [he wrote

from the China Sea], but the Lord our God in the midst of us is mighty—so we will trust and not be afraid. 'He will save.' He will save all the time and in everything."

And again, some months later, he wrote to Jenny:

"Flesh and heart often fail: let them fail! He faileth not. Pray very much, pray constantly, for Satan rages against us . . . There is much to distress. Your absence is a great and everpresent trial, and there is all the ordinary and extraordinary conflict. But the encouragements are also wonderful—no other word approaches the truth, and half of them cannot be told in writing. No one dreams of the mighty work going on in connection with our Mission. Other missions too, doubtless, are being greatly used. I look for a wonderful year."

When he sailed for China he planned to be back in England by the end of the year, but the unfinished work kept him into and through 1886—the most fruitful year the mission had yet experienced. Hudson spent months on an extensive inland tour, visiting new stations, instructing his missionaries, holding conferences, meeting with Chinese Christians, and even engaging in new evangelistic ventures. Old colleagues in distant stations, some he hadn't seen for years, shared old memories and rejoiced with Hudson at the exciting new growth of the mission. Younger missionaries found inspiration in the presence and the faithful example of the mission's leader. And in discussions with Hudson, they all dreamed and planned about the future of the work.

"We all saw visions at that time," recalled one missionary who traveled with Hudson. "Those were days of heaven upon earth. Nothing seemed difficult."

Hudson amazed his younger colleagues with his endurance as they traveled by foot and pack-mule over rugged terrain in the remotest regions of China. Often the inns where they stayed were so crude that the travelers shared sleeping quarters with their mules who would be so hungry they would eat the straw from the missionaries' pallets as they tried to sleep. Many times there were no inns to be found at all; and in the hottest weather the missionaries were sometimes forced to travel at night.

One young missionary, a noted athlete back in England, wrote about the rigors of Chinese travel:

"Night travelling was one of the hardest experiences I ever had, because I could not sleep by day. Occasionally, when I did drop off, I would wake to find that Mr. Taylor had been looking after me, rigging up mosquito netting to keep the flies away. Walking at night I have been so sleepy that even the motion could not keep me awake, and have fallen right down while plodding on—the tumble rousing one for the time being!

"The inns being closed at night, we used often to lie down by the roadside, when the animals had to be fed. Our own fare consisted chiefly of rice and millet. Occasionally we were able to purchase a chicken, eggs, cucumbers, or a little fruit. But we did not stop at regular stages, and as it was the rainy season, nothing was brought out for sale in the places through which we passed. With so much rain, we often got soaked through. The way we managed was to take off our garments one by one and dry them in front of the fire. On one occasion this so offended the 'Kitchen God' that Mr. Taylor had to come and make peace. Of course we carried no bedding, though Mr. Taylor always had two pillows, one for the head and one for the thigh, and we each carried a plaid. The medicine chest sometimes came in useful as an extra pillow . . .

"I remember coming to one river where there were a

few houses and people who made a harvest by carrying travellers over. They met us saying the river was impassable, nevertheless for a thousand cash apiece they would take us across. This was outrageous: so I went into the water which was rising by inches, the rain being a perfect deluge. When the men saw we were not to be deterred, they came and gave some help, glad to be paid a fair price for their work. After we were over, the water rose by feet. Had we been half an hour later, no crossing could have been possible. The river was by that time a wild, raging torrent.

"On the farther side there was a small village, but no inn. To go on was impossible. Stay we must, though the only shelter we could find was apparently a pig-sty. So we turned the occupant out, borrowed a few forms, took the doors off their hinges to lie on, and, rolling ourselves in our plaids, prepared to pass the night as comfortably as circumstances would admit. We were only masters of the situation for a short time, however; for the pig came back, charged the make-shift door, which at once fell in, and settled down to share the apartment with us. After reflection, I concluded that it was too cold to turn out on the chance of ignominious defeat at the hands of the enemy.

"Next day was still cold—high mountains instead of the Si-an plain, drenching rain instead of burning sun. The road was washed away in places, but still Mr. Taylor would push on. Where the riverside was impassable, we had to clamber up steep banks as best we could, and follow crumbling tracks on the mountains. Nothing would stop him, though he often begged me to remain behind. We had several narrow escapes from landslips—the path giving way behind us and rolling stones and earth into the stream.

Hudson Taylor's

We had no fear of robbers; and the wolves, though we saw them, did not attack us. We went 48 to 50 miles one day; and the last three stages we made in two, not to miss the mail [boat] at Han-chung."

Hearing Hudson sing on one occasion when the entire party was exhausted and extremely hungry, one of those with him noticed the words, "We thank Thee, Lord, for this our food," and couldn't help asking where the food was.

"It cannot be too far away," Hudson smiled. "Our Father knows we are hungry and will send our breakfast soon; but you will have to wait and say your grace when it comes, while I shall be ready to begin eating at once."

And sure enough, just ahead they met a man with ready-cooked rice to sell which made an excellent meal.

Even more impressive to those around him was Hudson's attention to spiritual nourishment. Whatever else he had to leave behind on his journey, he always carried a box of matches, candles, and his four-volume Bible.

"He would invariably get his quiet time an hour before dawn," one of his companions wrote. "And then possibly sleep again . . . when I woke to feed the animals I always found him reading the Bible by the light of his candle. No matter what the surroundings or the noise in those dirty inns, he never neglected this. He used to pray on such journeys lying down, for he usually spent long times in prayer, and to kneel would have been too exhausting."

The last segment of Hudson's great inland journey looked to be the easiest, a thousand-mile boat ride down the Han River from the northern provinces to the coast. But on this last stage of the trip, Hudson volunteered to take charge of Annie Pearse, the little five-year-old daughter of Han-chung missionaries who feared for the sickly girl's life. Her only hope seemed to be the changed climate at the coast.

Annie's parents, knowing there were no women in Hudson's party, worried about burdening him with their daughter's care for the four- to six-week journey. But Hudson insisted and personally saw to the child's clothes and meals on the trip—caring for her and watching over her day and night.

"My little charge is wonderfully improving [he was able to write Jenny from the boat]. She clings to me very lovingly, and it is sweet to feel little arms about one's neck once more."

No sooner did Hudson conclude his extensive tour of China than he convened the first meeting of the newly formed China Council of the mission. As 1886 drew to a close, the recently appointed superintendents of the provinces gathered at An-king where Hudson planned to share the results of his trip, discuss the most pressing needs of the mission, and then challenge the leaders of the mission in China to begin thinking about larger future developments.

But even Hudson was surprised when, after an entire week given to prayer and fasting, those attending the conference agreed that to make any significant advances at all, a hundred new workers were needed right away. A hundred! But as they carefully detailed the needs, Hudson had to agree that with fifty central stations already established, even a hundred new workers would be all too few for the new expansion they planned. So with Hudson's permission, the group cabled a message to London: "Praying for a hundred new workers in 1887."

What a stir that cable created in England. No mission in history had ever dreamed of sending out such an army of

Hudson Taylor's

missionary reinforcements. The China Inland Mission only had 190 members. People could hardly believe that they would pray for an increase of more than fifty percent in one year—until Hudson arrived home to tell of the three-part prayer being prayed by the missionaries in China.

Before he left, the mission leaders in China agreed to pray not just that God would bring them one hundred new workers, but also that, unsolicited, an extra fifty thousand dollars would be received above and beyond the present income so that all the new missionaries needs would be met. And third, that the extra money would come in large sums so that the small staff in the home office wouldn't be burdened with extra correspondence and recordkeeping.

And what happened in 1887? Six hundred men and women actually volunteered for service with the China Inland Mission during that year. One hundred two were chosen, equipped and sent out. Not just fifty thousand dollars but fifty-five thousand dollars in extra income was received, without solicitation, so that every need was met. Perhaps more amazingly, just eleven gifts covered it all, scarcely adding to the work of the staff.

Even so, the answers to prayer placed greater demands on Hudson. He spoke two, three, sometimes four times a day. He seemed to be constantly interviewing interested candidates and still managed a prodigious correspondence load averaging thirteen or fourteen letters a day, every day, for twelve months. But the story of "the Hundred" was told by Christians far and wide, creating even greater interest in China and the work of the mission.

As a result, Hudson was invited by Dwight L. Moody to stop in America on his way back to China in 1888. Hudson wrote:

"I had not the remotest idea in coming to America that

anything specially bearing upon the work of the China Inland Mission would grow out of it. I was glad to come when my way was providentially opened. I wanted to see Mr. Moody, and had heard of over two thousand students wishful to consecrate their lives to God's service abroad. The American societies, I thought, are not quite in a position to take up these two thousand, and perhaps if we tell them about God's faithfulness they will find it written in their Bibles not 'be sent' but 'go'. I believe in verbal inspiration, and that God could have said 'be sent' if he had wished it, instead of 'go'. I hoped I might be able to encourage some to 'go'."

After Hudson spoke to a large student conference Dr. Moody had organized, the inspired students took it upon themselves to raise money to be given as support for missionaries in China. The total amount of their giving was enough to pay the yearly expenses of eight missionaries.

But far from being joyous over this development, Hudson felt a new burden. As he explained:

"To have missionaries and no money would be no trouble to me for the Lord is bound to take care of His own: He does not want me to assume His responsibility. But to have money and no missionaries is very serious indeed. And I do not think it will be kind of you dear friends in America to put this burden upon us, and not to send some from among yourselves to use the money. We have the dollars, but where are the people?"

Hudson was anxious to get to China. And as he said, if he had missionaries without money he would be ready to leave immediately, trusting that the money would come. He had done just that on numerous occasions. But he couldn't just take the money and leave without the missionaries it was to support.

Moody encouraged Hudson to make a direct appeal for workers. So he did. And when the first three were accepted he began to feel glad about having the money in hand. But another complication developed. Every time he accepted another candidate, that person's friends, family, and church pledged to underwrite his support. So that when the first eight were chosen, the original fund remained untouched. It seemed to Hudson that consecrated money was something like consecrated loaves and fishes; there appeared to be no using it up.

So it was, though he had no previous intention to do so, that Hudson immediately established an American branch of the China Inland Mission and within only three months of his arrival sailed from the United States with fourteen young North American missionaries to China. From that time on, the China Inland Mission, which had always been interdenominational, was an international mission as well.

21

"If we can judge God's Word, instead of being judged by it, if we can give God as much or little as we like, then we are lords and He the indebted one, to be grateful for our dole and obliged by our compliance with His wishes. If on the other hand He is Lord, let us treat Him as such."

1889 - 1905

In the following years the China Inland Mission mushroomed into a truly worldwide ministry. Thirty-five Scandinavian missionaries, ready for service, arrived unannounced in Shanghai not long after Hudson had toured Norway and Sweden to speak about the spiritual needs of China. Germany sent contingents of workers for the mission, and Australia and New Zealand also joined in the work. Before long the China Council in Shanghai became the center of a greater organization than its founder had ever imagined.

But even though the spiritual overflow of his life's work now reached to the ends of the earth, even though his sense of responsibility and his work load grew in proportion, Hudson Taylor's faith held him up and kept him steady. Those around him noted his strength; and an Episcopalian minister who hosted him on a stay in Australia observed:

"He was an object lesson in quietness. He drew from the bank of heaven every farthing of his daily income—'My peace I give unto you.' Whatever did not agitate the Saviour or ruffle His spirit, was not to agitate him. The serenity of the Lord Jesus concerning any matter, and at its most crucial moment, was his ideal and practical possession. He knew nothing of rush or hurry, of quivering nerves or vexation of spirit. He knew that there is a peace passing all understanding, and that he could not do without it . . .

" 'I am in the study, you are in the big spare-room,' I said to Mr. Taylor at length. 'You are occupied with millions, I with tens. Your letters are pressingly important, mine of comparatively little moments. Yet I am worried and distressed, while you are always calm. Do tell me what makes the difference.'

" 'My dear Macartney,' he replied, 'the peace you speak of is, in my case, more than a delightful privilege, it is a necessity. I could not possibly get through the work I have to do without the peace of God "which passeth all understanding" keeping my heart and mind.'

"That was my chief experience of Mr. Taylor. Are you in a hurry, flurried, distressed? Look up! See the Man in the glory! Let the face of Jesus shine upon you—the wonderful face of the Lord Jesus Christ. Is He worried or distressed? There is no care on His brow, no least shade of anxiety. Yet the affairs are His as much as yours.

" 'Keswick teaching,' as it is called, was not new to me. I had received those glorious truths and was preaching them to others. But here was the real thing, an embodiment of 'Keswick teaching' such as I had never hoped to see. It impressed me profoundly. Here was a man almost sixty years of age, bearing tremendous burdens, yet absolutely calm and untroubled. Oh, the pile of letters! any one of which might contain news of death, of lack of funds, of riots or serious trouble. Yet all were opened, read, and answered with the same tranquility—Christ his reason for peace, his power for calm. Dwelling in Christ, he drew upon His very being and resources, in the midst of and concerning the matters in question. And this he did by an attitude of faith as simple as it was continuous.

Hudson Taylor's

"Yet he was delightfully free and natural. I can find no words to describe it save the scriptural expression 'in God.' He was in God all the time and God in him. It was that true 'abiding' of John 15. But oh, the lover-like attitude that underlay it! He had in relation to Christ a most bountiful experience of the Song of Solomon. It was a wonderful combination—the strength and tenderness of one who, amid stern preoccupation, like that of a judge on the bench, carried in his heart the light and love of home."

And through it all, the vision and spiritual urgency of his earlier years remained undimmed. In fact, his sense of responsibility to obey the last command of the Lord Jesus Christ only increased, as he came to see more clearly the meaning of the great commission. He wrote in 1889:

"I confess with shame that the question, what did our Lord really mean by His command to 'preach the gospel to every creature' had never been raised by me. I had laboured for many years to carry the Gospel further afield, as have many others; had laid plans for reaching every unevangelised province and many smaller districts in China, without realising the plain meaning of our Saviour's words.

"To every creature?"

There were only forty thousand Protestant Christians in all of China. Double that, triple the number, and suppose each one could take the message of the gospel to eight of his friends and neighbors. That would only be a million. The inadequacy of all his previous efforts convicted Hudson as he wrote:

"How are we going to treat the Lord Jesus Christ with regard to this last command? Shall we definitely drop the title 'Lord' as applied to Him? Shall we take the ground that we are quite willing to recognise Him as our Saviour, as far as the penalty of sin is concerned, but are not prepared to own ourselves 'bought with a price,' or Christ as having claim to our unquestioning obedience? . . .

"How few of the Lord's people have practically recognised the truth that Christ is either Lord of all or He is not Lord at all! If we can judge God's Word, instead of being judged by it, if we can give God as much or little as we like, then we are lords and He the indebted one, to be grateful for our dole and obliged by our compliance with His wishes. If on the other hand He is Lord, let us treat Him as such. 'Why call ye me, Lord, Lord, and do not the things which I say?' "

So it was that at sixty years of age, Hudson Taylor, missionary to all of inland China, broadened his mission's vision even farther. Nothing less would do but to begin a systematic effort to obey Jesus' command and share the story of His love and sacrifice with every man, woman, and child in all of China.

Jenny returned to China with Hudson in 1891, amazed at how much the mission had grown (and was still growing). As remarkable as it had seemed in 1887 when 100 missionaries went to China in one year, in 1890 and 1891 the China Inland Mission welcomed 131 new missionaries at Shanghai in less than six months' time—66 of them arriving in one three-week period. The history of Christian missions had seen nothing like it.

And the advances in China weren't limited to the work of the China Inland Mission. Between 1890 and 1895, 1153 new missionaries went to China through various mission agencies.

And the work continued to grow. By 1900 there were 750 China Inland Mission members. Four million dollars had been raised without anyone but God being asked to give, and there was no debt. Over 700 Chinese workers were connected with the mission and 13,000 Chinese believers had been baptized. Prospects for the brand new century looked even more exciting with the first steps begun in a deliberate strategy designed to reach every person in China with the gospel.

But then the Boxer Rebellion of 1900 broke out and its madness swept the country. With the official blessing of the Dowager Empress, the fanatical Boxers rose up from one end of China to the other in religious and patriotic fervor to drive out the "devil foreigners."

Hudson, his health broken during his tenth term of active missionary work in China (1898-1899), had at Jenny's insistence agreed to travel to Switzerland to rest and try to recuperate. They no sooner arrived there when the terrible word reached them.

Telegram after telegram came telling of riots, massacres, and the hunting down of refugees in station after station of the China Inland Mission. Each new word brought greater and greater sorrow until Hudson weakened emotionally and physically to the point that he thought he could bear no more. "I cannot read," he said at that point. "I cannot pray, I can scarcely even think—but I can trust."

Before the rebellion ended and order was restored in China, thousands died, including fifty-eight China Inland Mission members (along with twenty-one of their children), and countless Chinese converts of the mission. Yet when the violence did end, the China Inland Mission returned to its centers, many of which had been destroyed, and resumed the work without so much as a single demand to the Chinese government for compensation. That attitude of courage and forgiveness made an impression that helped set the stage for a new era of effective evangelism in China.

The words of a white-haired Chinese pastor in Shansi came true. "Kingdoms may perish," he said just before he was killed in the Boxer Rebellion, "but the Church of Christ can never be destroyed."

Hudson stepped down from the directorship of the mission in 1900, and his health prevented his return to China for some time. By the time he regained enough strength for another round-the-world journey, Jenny was herself dying of cancer. So he stayed and cared for her until she died in July, 1904.

During her last night, though she had obvious difficulty breathing, she kept assuring Hudson that she felt "no pain, no pain." But toward morning, seeing the anguish on his face, she finally whispered, "Ask Him to take me quickly."

Never had Hudson prayed such a difficult prayer; but for his wife's sake he asked God to free her spirit. Within five minutes Jenny's breathing grew quieter. And then all was peace.

Hudson's sense of desolation was unspeakable. On the wall of the Taylor sitting-room hung a Scripture text—the last purchase the couple had made together. Many times in the days following Jenny's death, Hudson looked up through his tears to those words in blue on their white background: *"Celui qui a fait les prommesses est fidele."* (Faithful is He who made the promises.) He told a friend, "All we have to do is look out with patience to see how He will prove it true."

Early the following year Hudson sailed with his son and daughter-in-law to China. At seventy-three years of age, he made a long, remarkable tour of the country that took him to many familiar spots and even into the province of Hunan where he had never journeyed before.

Hudson Taylor's

And oh, how the people responded—both missionaries and the Chinese—everywhere he went. He was called "Venerable Father" and "Benefactor of China" by many who came to greet him. Crowds gathered to hear him whenever he spoke and sometimes just to see him pass.

The trip into Hunan had to be especially gratifying. It was the last of the provinces to get a permanent China Inland Mission station. And it hadn't been fully accessible until after the Boxer Rebellion. Hudson was anxious to see that part of the country. And as his party crossed the wide expanse of Tong-ting Lake and steamed upriver toward the capital of Chang-sha, he couldn't help but have thought about all the toil and prayer that had gone into opening up that last province of China to the gospel. Less than ten years before, not one missionary had settled there. Now there were no fewer than 111 from 13 different mission agencies, with work in 17 different cities and a strong band of Chinese Christians working along with them. The advances were indeed remarkable.

"A work of God" was the only way people could think to describe the impact of Hudson Taylor's life and of the China Inland Mission. But Hudson's response was summed up in his words, "We cannot do much, but we can do a little, and God can do a great deal."

On Saturday, June 3, 1905, the missionaries in Hunan's capital city welcomed Hudson with a reception. That evening his daughter-in-law went into his room to check on him.

"Dear Father was in bed, the lamp burning on the chair beside him, and he was leaning over it with his pocket-book lying open and the home letters it contained spread out as he loved to have them. I drew the pillow up more comfortably under his head, and sat down on a low chair close beside him. As he said nothing, I began talking a little about the pictures in the *Missionary Review* lying open on the bed . . . and I was just in the middle of a sentence when dear Father turned his head quickly and gave a little gasp. I looked up, thinking he was going to sneeze. But another came, then another. He was not choking or distressed for breath. He did not look at me or seem conscious of anything.

"I ran to the door and called Howard [his son], but before he could reach the bedside it was evident that the end had come. I ran back to call Dr. Keller, who was just at the foot of the stairs. In less time than it takes to write it he was with us, but only to see dear Father draw his last breath. It was not death—but the glad, swift entry upon life immortal.

". . . and oh, the look of rest and calm that came over the dear face was wonderful! The weight of years seemed to pass away in a few moments. The weary lines vanished. He looked like a child quietly sleeping, and the very room seemed full of unutterable peace."

Epilogue

Hudson Taylor's body was taken, in a casket generously purchased by poor Chinese Christians from the province of Hunan, to the family plot in a little cemetery in Chin-kiang. There his body was buried beside those of his wife and children on the banks of the mighty Yangtze River, in the heart of the land he loved and lived and died for.

And what was to become of the China Inland Mission? Hudson Taylor had been a man of such unusual faith; God had always blessed the mission while he lived and prayed for it. But what now?

Hudson Taylor's legacy lived on and continued to grow through the ministry of the China Inland Mission. By the time the Japanese invaded China during the 1930s in the first stages of the Second World War, the mission's membership had swelled to 1285. The total income since 1900 had reached $20 million unsolicited; there were between three and four thousand Chinese workers with the mission; and the baptisms in the first three decades of the 1900s had totalled more than one hundred thousand.

The China Inland Mission, like all Christian organizations, was expelled from China when Mao Tse-tung and his communists took over the country after World War II. But the mission continues today under the name of Overseas Missionary Fellowship with its headquarters in Singapore, and over one thousand missionaries serving in nine countries throughout Southeast Asia. And the China Inland Mission's impact, like that of Hudson Taylor himself, lives on today in Communist China.

Despite the repressive decades of communist persecution, the Chinese church, just as during the Boxer Rebellion, "could not be destroyed." So that when Western Christians regained a measure of access to inland China again in the seventies and eighties, the worldwide Christian church learned there were by then millions of Chinese Christians and thousands of house-churches throughout China. And many, if not most of those millions of Chinese Christians must trace their Christian heritage back to the work of the China Inland Mission and its spiritual father, Hudson Taylor.

What was the secret of this spiritual giant's strength? What enabled his life to make such an impact?

Part of his secret was expressed in the words to one of his favorite verses:

He told me of a river bright
That flows from Him to me,
That I might be, for His delight,
A fair and fruitful tree.

Tersteegen

"It is very simple," he wrote. "But has He not planted us by the river of living water that we may be, for His delight, fair and fruitful to His people?"

God came first in Hudson Taylor's life—not the work, not the needs of China or of the mission, not his own experiences. He knew that the promise was true, "Delight thyself also in the Lord, and he shall give thee the desires of thine heart."

From a practical standpoint, he knew the truth of Oswald Chambers's statement: "God does not give us overcoming life; he gives us life as we overcome." And to Hudson Taylor, the secret of overcoming lay in daily, hourly fellowship with God. This, he learned, could only be maintained by personal prayer and faithful meditation on God's Word.

With the life he lived, and its demands on his time and energy, finding opportunity for his own spiritual maintenance wasn't easy. But he made it a priority.

On his last journey through China with his son and daughter-in-law, they traveled month after month through northern China by cart and by wheelbarrow; the inns they stayed in by night offered only the crudest accommodations. Often, when there would be only one large room for everyone spending the night in that inn, his children would screen off a portion of the room for their father with curtains of some sort. Then, after everyone was asleep, they would be awakened to the sound of a match striking and see the flicker of candlelight which told them Hudson was awake and reading his Bible. From 2 a.m. to 4 a.m. was his usual prayer time—the time he could count on being undisturbed in prayer. And that flicker of candlelight said more to his children about prayer than anything they ever read or heard on the subject.

The hardest part of a missionary career, Hudson Taylor admitted, was to maintain regular, prayerful Bible study. "Satan will always find you something to do," he would say, "when you ought to be occupied about that, if it is only arranging a window blind."

So he would have fully agreed with the words of Andrew Murray who wrote:

"Take time. Give God time to reveal Himself to you. Give yourself time to be silent and quiet before Him, waiting to receive, through the Spirit, the assurance of His presence with you, His power working in you. Take time to read His word as in His presence, that from it you may know what He asks of you and what He promises you. Let the Word create around you, create within you a holy atmosphere, a holy heavenly light, in which your soul will be refreshed and strengthened for the work of daily life."

That's just what Hudson Taylor did. For when he was over seventy years of age he paused, Bible in hand, as he crossed his sitting-room at home, and said to one of his children: "I have just finished reading the Bible through, today, for the fortieth time in forty years."

And he not only read it, he lived it. Hudson Taylor stopped at no sacrifice in following Christ. "Cross-loving men are needed," he wrote in the midst of his labors in China. And if he could speak to us today he would no doubt say again:

"There is a needs-be for us to give ourselves for the life of the world. An easy, non-self-denying life will never be one of power. Fruit-bearing involves cross-bearing. There are not two Christs—an easy-going one for easy-going Christians, and a suffering, toiling one for exceptional believers. There is only one Christ. Are you willing to abide in Him, and thus to bear much fruit?"

Note to the Reader

The publisher invites you to share your response to the message of this book by writing Discovery House Publishers, P.O. Box 3566, Grand Rapids, MI 49501, U.S.A. or by calling 1-800-283-8333. For information about other Discovery House publications, contact us at the same address and phone number.

This book is also available from OMF Books:
2 Cluny Road, Singapore 1025, Republic of Singapore;
404 South Church Street, Robesonia, PA 19551, U.S.A.;
1058 Avenue Road, Toronto, ON M5N 2C6, Canada;
and at other Overseas Missionary Fellowship centers.